PRAYING WITH FEMININE
IMAGES OF GOD

Called
Into
Her
Presence

Virginia Ann Froehle, R.S.M.

AVE MARIA PRESS   Notre Dame, Indiana 46556

© 1992 by Ave Maria Press, Notre Dame, IN 46556

All rights reserved. No part of this book may be used or reproduced in any manner whatsoever without written permission, except in the case of reprints in the context of reviews.

International Standard Book Number: 0-87793-470-3

Library of Congress Catalog Card Number: 91-75852

Cover photograph by Cleo Freelance Photo.

Cover and text design by Katherine Robinson Coleman.

Printed and bound in the United States of America.

To my sister
Theresa Froehle Ganote,
whose faithful love has reflected to me
the unconditional embrace
of God
as Sister, Mother, and Friend.

CONTENTS

Introduction 7

PART ONE
Called Into Her Presence 17

PART TWO
Praying With Feminine Images of God:
Exercises, Experiences, and Celebrations *37*

Loving Oneself in the Present Moment 39

Trust in Her 49

Receiving Her Forgiveness 61

Mirroring Her 73

Imaging Her 87

Kneading, Baking, and Breaking Prayer 97

Serving Her Through Love and Justice 109

APPENDIX A
Openers to Connect With One Another 125

APPENDIX B
Resource Guide 131

INTRODUCTION

When I began to explore feminine images of God in prayer, I leaped forward in my walk in the Spirit. I continue to move gladly in this relationship with God as Her—as well as with God as Him. This book flows from my ongoing desire and efforts to do so.

I invite you also to open yourself to new images of God and to new experiences in prayer arising from them. May you come to know the warmth and depth of God's feminine embrace. May you also come to understand more fully how our images of God affect not only our prayer, but also our lives in community with one another.

My first discovery was that praying personally with feminine images of God enhances prayer and, therefore, relationship to God. Then I began to realize that when I joined others in praying with feminine images, we started perceiving our place in political, religious, economic, and social systems differently. Our present images of God reflect the history of these systems and reinforce them. New images can modify them. Praying with feminine as well as masculine images of God calls us to greater gender equality "on earth as it is in heaven."

Searching for feminine images puts our feet on a path virtually untouched in modern times. Walking the path asks, however, the instincts of a mother as we bring new images to birth and nurture them with creativity and patience. Trust that your exploration will lead you to a fuller knowledge of who God is so that you can give yourself to a greater love of God, yourself, and others—in full spiritual maturity.

Most people who choose to walk this path stroll along slowly. Persons who are growing in faith evolve new images of God fairly regularly. Yet prayer is often more difficult during these periods. Everyone needs time to integrate new images of God. A few persons, however, do leap and dance forward when they discover the feminine of themselves as one with the feminine of God. They find new freedom in the gifts of the new images.

Evolving Images of God Is Challenging

Often people remember their first impressions and images of God as "a cloud in the sky," "a grandfatherly man with a beard," "an eye looking at me," "an old man on a throne." Getting these images together as children was quite a task. Changing and modifying these images later is also a challenge.

I have offered over a hundred retreat days or evenings of praying with feminine images. "I can't get an image. I can't picture what God looks like as a woman," is often the complaint of someone who is making a first attempt at praying with a feminine image. Or, "I keep seeing Mary, not God." Many of us are used to a visual masculine image of God when we pray and so we look for its counterpart. In this confusion we become like children. Recall their questions when they first hear of God: "What does God look like?" "Is God big?" "What does God do all day?" "Does God have a television?" Children struggle to get some inner pictures of someone they cannot see.

Unfortunately, the only gender images we learned as children were masculine ones. When we decide to pray with feminine ones, we need to start all over. We need to explore each image not only visually, but also emotionally—sensing the impact it has on us— consolation, confusion, fear, peace, and so on. We need time to "get it together" again.

As you pray and meditate with the suggestions in this book, perhaps you will feel encouraged to look for other feminine images and will continue to experiment with other forms of prayer. Whenever you and I come together to share prayer that celebrates such images, we can reveal the feminine image of our God shrouded by centuries of patriarchy. We see God and ourselves more clearly.

Images Can Go Beyond Pictures

An image of God may be visual. It may also be a sensed presence that carries no picture with it. We all form images with our inner eye, our imagination, and also with our "sixth sense." Visual imagination creates pictures for us—a person, light, a cloud, a flame. But the imagination can also sense a presence without seeing anything, as you do when you know someone is in the room behind you even though the person did not make a sound. You sense a presence even if you don't know who it is—and feel an emotion toward the unknown presence. If you believe the presence to be someone you love, you feel warm and relaxed.

If you identify the unseen presence in the room as your father, the feelings evoked are different from those of recognizing the presence as your mother. Just the words *mother* and *father* elicit distinct feelings. If you know only that the unseen presence is male or that it is female, this awareness will also affect your reaction. Sensing God's presence as masculine or feminine calls up different responses. This is why adding the feminine of God to our prayer expands the content and emotional range of the prayer. We experience other possibilities for relationship.

Using Feminine Images When Praying With Scripture

Praying with feminine images in scripture surfaces questions and creates problems. The biggest problem is that masculine images dominate the writings and, therefore, unconsciously reinforce our unjust social structures. Some feminists choose to avoid the problem by avoiding the Bible. This book suggests some other alternatives.

We can view patriarchy—the rule of men in religion, economics, politics, and society—at the time the Hebrew scriptures were written in the same way we view slavery as a part of the system when the Christian scriptures were written. The overriding subject of the scriptures is the relationship, action, and presence of God in *men's* lives. This fact reflects the patriarchal structure. If we collected all the books and passages that emphasize the action and presence of God in *women's* lives, we would have slim pickings! But the purpose of the scriptures is not to give religious sanction to patriarchy any more than it is to claim legitimacy for slavery.

The male images of God as father, king, warrior, and judge come from the patriarchal society and dominate the pages of the Bible. Feminine images of God also exist—in the Song of Songs, Deutero-Isaiah, Hosea, and others. But because women and feminine qualities were downplayed in the culture, these images are exceptions. Few as they are, however, they are a legitimate part of our tradition.

We have come to accept historical and scientific inaccuracies in the Bible, knowing that the purpose of scripture is not to teach history or science. God's power in the scriptures is in giving us messages about God's relationship with us, even though these may be expressed with the cultural biases of the authors, for example, recording them from a male perspective. Knowing that the purpose of the Bible is not to teach that God is male or that patriarchy is a divine institution, we can feel free to experiment—in private or small-group prayer—with substituting feminine images for masculine ones. We can use the scriptures to look at God's actions in our lives—whether male or female—from a feminine perspective.

Balancing Our Masculine and Feminine Images

My hope is to expand images of God, to balance masculine and feminine. Yet, I have not balanced them in this book. The feminine has hardly even begun to gain balance in the world. We are just begining to learn to pray to our God as feminine. So I toss this book as one drop of the feminine into the sea of masculine-God oriented prayer books. The balance I dream about is broader than that of a single book.

Using capital letters for the pronouns referring to God and Jesus is out of fashion among editors. But I choose to use them. Using She and Her—as well as He and Him—emphasizes the feminine and that is part of the book's purpose. The emphasis challenges us as we adopt and claim new images. Some people, I realize, find the emphasis disturbing. I invite those of you who do so to work through the emotional reasons for this. (I have had to do so also.) It is an opportunity for understanding yourself better and for expanding your awareness—whether or not you ever choose to pray with feminine images.

Depth and richness of prayer, expanding your relationship with God, is the gift I wish for you through these prayer experiences, exercises, and celebrations. May you know a new freedom to explore and to grow in love.

Using This Book

This book will help you to explore seven prayer themes: accepting and loving yourself, learning to trust, accepting God's forgiveness, seeing others and yourself as gifts made in the image of our God, finding out who you are in God right now, examining the ways you affect others and the ways they affect you, and discovering your way of making the world a better place.

Within each theme are six different methods of praying: an *Opening Prayer*, a *Guided Imagery Meditation*, *For Personal Prayer* (exercises), a *Psalm Parallel*, a *Personal Ritual*, and a *Common (Group) Ritual*.

You can use any of these ways of praying as an individual. The prayers are arranged by themes so that groups can also use them to plan a day or an evening of prayer together.

Using This Book for Personal Prayer

Choose one theme. Before you begin to pray, find a time and place with the least probability of distraction. Take time to relax. Close your eyes, relax all the parts of your body, and visualize something or some place that is pleasing. Or, if a beautiful object is near you, rest your eyes on each part of it and the whole of it. Being relaxed in and before God is as important as being relaxed with a spouse or a friend.

Call to your consciousness the presence of God within you or near you or surrounding you. Be aware that this presence is feminine. If you do not experience this, ask God for it as a gift.

Then pray the short *Opening Prayer* within your heart or aloud. As you do so, linger with the phrases or thoughts you find most comfortable.

The *Guided Imagery Meditations* carry their own relaxation exercises. You may wish to read the meditations at your own pace. Or you can be guided in those meditations by listening to them on audiocassettes (see Froehle, Appendix B). The meditations on the tapes are the same as the ones in this book except for some slight adaptations made for smooth reading.

You may find writing answers to the reflection/discussion questions at the end of each meditation useful. Writing demands that we clarify our thoughts. Undefined conflicts or cloudy insights often come into focus on paper. If you find writing a chore, try other ways of getting a clear hold on your thoughts and feelings. You might try talking, drawing, painting, clay modeling, gestures, or dance. God's work is most fully expressed when we use the gifts and preferences God has given us.

Some may find the suggestions in *For Personal Prayer* to be new ways of praying. If you are adventurous enough to have chosen this book for your prayer, you are probably willing to experiment with some new methods of praying.

The *Psalm Parallel* is a contemporary psalm inspired by the thoughts, words, and rhythms of a biblical psalm. Take some time to sample random psalms within the Hebrew scriptures and look for feminine touches. You will find a few, but not many. You will discover that they generally sound as if they are written to a male God about masculine concerns. In *Psalm Parallels* you will be praying with a female image of God about feminine concerns. I hope you will write new psalms from your own experience and incorporate feminine images of God.

Each *Personal Ritual* is a symbolic action to express an experience, insight, or feeling. When you perform a ritual, the actions you choose not only express what is in your heart but also enhance your grasp and experience of it.

Ritual involves your senses, your hands, your body—as well as your mind, your heart, your words. Entering into prayer with more of yourself can lead you to experience your relationship to God more fully.

Rituals can be communal or personal experiences. The most helpful personal rituals are ones created to express a particular moment in relationship to God, others, or oneself. If, after praying and meditating on a theme, you think of an action to express your prayer or relationship, do it. This may be as simple as placing a wild flower on a windowsill or sending a rose to someone. You may choose to place a stone on your dresser, tape a word to your bathroom mirror, bake a loaf of bread, or write a phrase or two to go under a magnet in your car or on your refrigerator. Perhaps you'll feel inspired to draw a picture and put it in a prominent place—or in a secret place. A *Personal Ritual* for each theme has been suggested. Feel free to use it or create your own.

Using This Book in a Group

Called Into Her Presence encourages active participation. Listening to long readings, praying extensively with another person's words, or long periods of just watching promote passivity. These prayers and rituals invite participants to be as active as they are willing to be. Words and actions for a leader are meant to help facilitate, not dominate, a group.

If you are planning a day of prayer, make certain that any publicity states clearly that participants will be praying with feminine images of God or exploring prayer using feminine images. Some people may come eagerly; others with some degree of curiosity and skepticism. Show the skeptics that you accept them. Welcome their questions or objections. Give them room to learn.

If those who come, open as they may be, do not understand some of the personal, societal, and political reasons for praying with feminine images, you will need to allow some time for explanation, discussion, and questions. "Why Pray With Feminine Images?" on page 19 provides background. One or several persons could absorb the information on these pages and offer it in their own words. Or some persons could acquaint themselves with the information and just answer the questions that arise.

You may wish to ask one person to read the *Opening Prayer* that begins each theme section, or you may ask group members to pray it together.

Select someone with a soothing voice to read the *Guided Imagery Meditation*. A person who has never before led this kind of prayer should practice with listeners to find a good reading pace. Or play the recording of the meditation in *In Her Presence: Prayer Experiences Exploring Feminine Images of God* (see Froehle, Appendix B).

Follow the meditation with some reflection/discussion questions, choosing those appropriate for your group. Because this activity is usually most successful, most fruitful, when it happens in small groups, break into groups of four to eight. Afterward, when the small groups have merged again into a large group, ask the participants to volunteer statements about feelings, difficulties, insights, and so on. Do not argue or contradict any statements. Look at each speaker and acknowledge each verbal statement with a thank you. If someone has a serious problem or conflict, do not try to resolve it in the group. Suggest talking about it later. One or two of the planners, or someone with good listening skills, should approach the person in the hours that follow and offer him or her the opportunity to talk further.

The *For Personal Prayer* section usually offers participants several choices. As a leader or planner you may want to choose one suggestion for the group and ask everyone to pray from it. Or you may want to let each person choose one of the suggestions. Allow enough time for everyone to find a place and get settled, in addition to time for prayer. Twenty minutes is a slim minimum; forty minutes is the maximum unless you have regular, experienced meditators used to longer periods of quiet prayer each day.

Many people benefit from reflecting on their prayer and articulating their experiences, favorable or unfavorable. Some people need to remain quiet and prefer not to share their thoughts. Provide some options following the *For Personal Prayer* time, for example, small-group sharing, one person sharing with another, private time for further reflection, being part of a group as a listener only. Generally fifteen minutes for this is sufficient.

The *Psalm Parallels* may be copied and distributed (one-time use only) so that participants may use them for private prayer. If each person has a Bible, you might suggest certain psalms and ask members of the group to pray these, substituting a feminine image of God for a masculine one. (Suggestions: Psalm 66, 68 [vs. 1–6], 93, 95, 96, 100.) If your group members enjoy being creative, ask them to write their own psalm parallel.

A *Common Ritual* is often the most moving part of a day and should be reserved for the closing. It is also the most challenging to plan.

Ideally a ritual should flow from the day—what has happened in the group, the content shared, feelings expressed, conflicts resolved or unresolved. It should signify the day's journey as a group yet give room for individual expression. Some people would say that rituals should not be planned but should *emerge* from the group experience. Some group leaders are able to pull this off, but not many. Most of us need to have something in mind, something prepared. We may then be able to modify this to make it even more appropriate to the experience of the day.

In using the *Common Ritual* you will need to assess what your particular group members find comfortable, a bit uncomfortable but all right to try, or unacceptable. Some people may find a particular symbol and action enriching; others may find the same symbol and action empty.

Prepare for the *Common Ritual* with the knowledge you have of the group at the planning time and gather the materials needed. At the end of five or six hours together, the group may be ready for much more than anyone could have asked of them at the beginning of the day. The trust level may be considerably higher. Still, you may find some people who are still uneasy about the day (or their lives), and some who set themselves apart. Or the day may have been fruitful for many individuals but little happened to the group as a whole. So be prepared to add to, subtract from, and modify the ritual.

A Creative God Is With You

Our God is a creative God. You are made in God's image and likeness. God wants you to be creative. Your relationship with God can then continually deepen and grow.

PART ONE

*Called
Into
Her
Presence*

Called Into Her Presence

Why Pray With Feminine Images?

God is spirit. God is neither male nor female—any more than God is fire, rock, shepherd, shield, wind, king, light, or any other image we project. The images we choose for God, however, affect our relationship with God. They modify our view of ourselves and others. They even affect our political, social, and economic systems. The God-images we inherit and those we choose to use in prayer shape our lives.

To illustrate this, can you give yourself permission to imagine a church that pictures God differently than our present churches do? Consider how such a church might have influenced you while you were growing up. Or consider how a boy or a girl born this morning and raised in this environment would be affected. Here is a word-picture of such a world:

> When people sing in church, they praise God's faithfulness, Her queenship and power over the universe, Her protective care. Sermons call everyone to be grateful to Her, to trust in Her motherly love and to live by Her commands. Church windows and paintings present Her sometimes as a woman on a throne, sometimes as a lover reaching out Her arms, sometimes as the center and source of creation surrounded with the moon and stars, animals, trees, birds, and human beings.

Leaders of the Eucharist are always women and every Mass is publicly offered for the salvation of all women or womankind. Men are included, of course, and are told so from the time they are small. After all, the words *woman* and *women* contain the words *man* and *men*. The lectors address church readings to everyone as "My sisters in Christ," and ritual passages use many phrases like "women of God."

Some men and women want to change the feminine-only image of God or the use of *women* for both sexes or the calling forth of women only for priestly leadership. They are told that women more perfectly reflect the image of God as seen in the qualities of Jesus who was eminently noncompetitive, gentle, nurturing, understanding, nonviolent, and forgiving. The word *woman* is, therefore, more appropriate. It is God's will that women be Her chief ministers of the gospel.

If you had grown up in a church like that, how would it have influenced you? How would such an environment affect a child born this year and raised in it? Would it influence the way a young boy learns to think of himself and his relationship to girls, then to women? How would it affect a girl? Would society change in any way? Would people's sense of God be different? their prayer?

If you feel uneasy, irritated, angry, or delighted with this fantasy, you are among those who recognize intuitively the power of words and images. Nothing carries our attitudes, prejudices, and values from generation to generation more clearly.

As we examine our present masculine-only words and images of God, we are called to ask ourselves what attitudes and values they leave with us. How do they prejudice us? What values are we handing down to our children and grandchildren? In the light of your conclusions about the fantasy, how do you think the present words and images—the reversal of the fantasy—are affecting our people and society?

I hope you do feel irritated or anxious or angry about such a scenario. Such a fantasy holds no more justice or truth than the all-male version of God and religious leadership we have had for centuries. It is just reverse discrimination. So I certainly would never want this to happen. I believe that God desires equality and mutual service, not dominance of any group over another.

Ancient Religion Saw God in a Feminine Image

Images of God have not always been masculine. In fact, humans have actually envisioned and worshiped God as a woman much longer than as a man. Scientists have unearthed countless statues of females, statues that held positions of honor in homes and shrines. Scholars first thought these were a variety of goddesses to whom people prayed for fertility in their families, their animals, and their crops. More recent studies in archeology and anthropology, however, reveal that they do not represent a variety of goddesses. They image a Goddess as the dominant deity, one whose dominion encompassed far more than fertility.

This feminine God had different names in different cultures. The Divine Presence was *Nut* in Egypt, *Siva* in Russia, *Nammu* in Sumaria, *Eurynome* in Greece and so on—all female names. For about twenty thousand years, the people of these regions worshiped the Great Holy One as feminine.

In the period which followed (about 7000–2000 B.C.E.) people continued to worship God—or the highest of the gods—as female in the cultures of Europe, England, Ireland, Wales, the Mediterranean (including northern Africa), large parts of Russia, India, and other parts of the Near East. Among Her titles were Queen of the Universe, Mother of All Creation, Queen Above All Gods. Cities of the Mediterranean area during this period were well-developed and highly complex. Many built around temples to such a goddess were cultural centers of the world.

In contrast to the peoples who thought of God as feminine, many other peoples in other areas of the world spoke of and prayed to God as if God were masculine.

Does a people's image of God make a difference? Yes. It seems that thinking of God as male or female had powerful political and social implications.

Many of the cultures who worshiped a feminine God also focused on women's contributions as more essential. Their societies were largely agrarian, and women's knowledge and skills in cultivating, preserving, and healing were at the heart of survival and growth. Women were honored because they had the power of giving birth; they were at the center of family, commerce, and religion. In many places women not only owned land, but passed it on through their daughters. Women had or shared responsibility for business and trade. Because they were perceived to image God, they were the religious leaders of the temples. They had freedom, prestige, and choice in their lives. The feminine image of God reflected these qualities of the societies and reinforced them.

In contrast, the masculine-God worshipers came from harsher climates where the meat and skins of hunted or herded animals were the source of survival, growth, and prosperity. Their societies heralded the physical strength and skills of men. These groups had become patriarchies, societies in which only men could rule or become mediators of the Divine. Men controlled commerce, property—and women. The masculine image of God reflected these societies and reinforced them.

Masculine-God Worshipers Conquer

The male-ruled groups invaded the feminine-God worshiping societies during a five-thousand-year period. They conquered and settled in their territories. Sometimes male-God and female-God worshipers blended aspects of their societies and religions. Both deities "married" and reigned equally. As patriarchy became stronger, however, the male deity became the superior God. Eventually, the feminine figure was demoted from sovereignty to being a caretaker of some area of specialty such as fertility or the underworld.

Myths tell the story of this change as a masculine hero slays a dragon or large snake, the symbol of the feminine God's wisdom and knowledge of the underworld and Her power over birth, death, and rebirth. By 500 C.E. most groups and shrines dedicated to the feminine Life-Giver had been destroyed.

The clash between conquerors and conquered was not just between two images of God, but between two social and political systems, between two kinds of role relationships between men and women. As these changed after the invasions, so did people's ways of picturing their God(s). Then, as they worshiped according to their new images of God, they reinforced their new social structures—those of patriarchy.

The Hebrew tribes, who were among those who invaded the Near East at the end of this period (about 2000 B.C.E.), were

strongly patriarchal. Their all-male priesthood (the Levites) con-
demned any feminine images as treacherous, as "an abomination."
The image of God as a woman challenged their whole social and
political system of male domination. These tribes destroyed whole
peoples who still worshiped a female God—or any other God
whose image differed from the one they honored.

Those who wrote down the stories of attack, battle, and
slaughter some fourteen hundred years later, in what we now call
the historical books of the Bible, said that God commanded their
leaders to slaughter these people when they took over their lands.
The "true God," they said, wanted all "false gods" destroyed.

It is important to realize that when people are condemning
a "false god," they are actually rejecting someone else's *image* of
God. Religious leaders—then and today—may say, "Our God is
the one true God." But what they are really saying is, "Our image
of God is better than your image of God. Our *image* is the true
one. Yours is false."

The Hebrews' words and images have influenced the whole
Western world's way of looking at God. Through the Bible, the
most widely read book of the West, the Hebrew masculine God is
most often presented as warrior, king, and judge—although He is
sometimes pictured as a lover, a redeemer, and a caring parent.
Once in a great while we find in the Bible a feminine image of
God.

Effect of Early Religious Education

In most religion classes today children hear of God only as
"Him." Most of us grew up with pictures of God as a grandfather
with a long white beard, holding the tablets of the command-
ments. How many impressions of God have been influenced by
the muscular Creator on the Sistine Chapel ceiling? or the shepherd carrying home a lost lamb on a picture that has hung in many
homes?

In the church priests and people address God as if God were
an exalted man or a super man. Parish congregations sing to God
as lord, father, king, and military leader marching at the head
of soldiers going to war against evil. Hymns praise "Him." The
persons of the Trinity are described as two males—Father and

Son—and a Spirit who is theologically genderless. Songs, hymns, and homilies, however, tell of this Spirit using "His power," "His anointing," and the Nicene Creed uses all male pronouns for this third person. So most people grow up *feeling* that God is male, even though most *know* that God is spirit.

Jesus Is Male

Few human beings can envision and relate to total spirit. Most of us need concrete images for God. For example, addressing God as a rock emphasizes God's constant, unchanging presence. Seeing God as a shield highlights God's protection. Picturing God as a shepherd reinforces the sense of God's continual care. In theology we learn that Jesus is the ultimate image of God, showing us more fully the qualities of our God. Many people say they can imagine Jesus and relate better to Him than they can to God as Spirit.

This need for concreteness and analogy leads some to confuse the *image* of God with God. Few people today would confuse a rock or a shield or a shepherd with God. But some do contend that if Jesus is *the* image of God (and since He *is* God), God must be male.

Does Jesus image God in his male physical sexuality? Or in His total goodness, open reverence for each person and all of creation, personal care, desire to heal and forgive—qualities that all human beings are able to possess? Moreover, doesn't Jesus offer the world His androgyny—the balance of the masculine and feminine in one human being? He is physically male and has many of the so-called masculine qualities, but He also eminently radiates the so-called feminine ones.

We see this masculine Jesus teaching with authority, living a rugged life traveling the countryside with His friends, defending God's house from thieves. Yet His nurturing presence, care for others, forgiveness, open show of emotions, emphasis on love of one another rather than competition are among the so-called feminine qualities. Has any other human being had such a perfect balance of masculine and feminine? In 1 Corinthians 1:25 we read that Christ is "the power of God and the wisdom of God." Power is a quality most associated with masculine in the scripture.

Wisdom is *Sophia* in Greek, the most frequently used word in the Bible next to God and Jesus; and *Sophia*, wisdom, is feminine.

God as a Special Kind of Parent

Some people point out Jesus spoke of God as His Father. Jesus did teach His disciples to pray by addressing God as "Our Father." We must remember, though, that the image of God as Father existed before Jesus used it. In his society the patriarchal father had power and authority over the household and could do with people and things as he willed. Jesus changed this authoritarian image of God as Father to a Father who is gentle, loving, and caring. He used the word *abba* and urged His followers to pray as if they were talking to someone who loves them as a daddy loves.

He said that God is like a close and nurturing parent—not a distant, authoritarian, judgmental one. Our God is one who cares when a child needs food and clothing, understands when a son's or daughter's feelings are hurt, is ready to forgive—even the adult child who stumbles and falls. God is *like* that, Jesus teaches, like *that kind* of father, *that kind* of parent. Jesus wasn't saying that God is a biological father, that God has a body or that God is male. He was telling us about the kind of child-parent relationship we are to assume with God.

In other places the biblical authors address God in metaphors as "my fortress" (Ps 31:4), "my light" (Ps 27:1), and speak of God's "mighty arm" and "right hand" (Ps 89:14). Jesus says, "I am the bread of life" (Jn 6:35) and "I am the vine" (Jn 15:5), among other figures of speech. We do not equate God or Jesus with any of those poetic words. Nor do we equate God with maleness because we use father as metaphor.

Jesus uses many figures of speech for Himself and for God. He describes God as a shepherd who goes in search of one lost sheep (Lk 15:3–7). Following that passage He compares God to the homemaker who searches for a lost coin (Lk 15:8–10). God is *like* a shepherd. God is *like* a housewife. God is *like* a man. God is *like* a woman.

Each image helps, yet also limits knowledge of God. Each image presents one or two facets of God—but only one or two—at a time. That is why using many images can expand our knowledge of an infinite God. Praying with a variety of images can foster a deeper relationship as the pray-er comes to experience more of God's "personality," which we picture through comparisons and likenesses.

The Feminine God in the Bible

We learned our basic mental pictures of God from the Bible or from hearing bible stories. Some popular biblical images that we absorbed are God as a father, a judge, a warrior, a king, a shepherd, and a lord. Yet the Bible also pictures God as a seamstress, a woman in labor, a female eagle, a woman who wipes away tears from another's face, and a gentle nursing mother. We heard little or nothing of these images.

The feminine images are not plentiful. Yet they are part of the word of God. They have legitimacy in our tradition. But since those who choose the passages to be read at Mass have largely skipped over them, we must search for them ourselves.

Sometimes, with the help of some scholars, we discover words for God whose visual image is genderless, but whose grammar is feminine. In Genesis 1:2 we read that the earth was a wasteland covered with darkness when *ruah* (a feminine noun sometimes translated "spirit," sometimes "wind") swept over the waters and began to create all that is and lives upon our earth.

The Hebrew word for *the Word of God* is the feminine *torah*. In Psalm 33:6 we read, "By the word of the LORD [*torah*] the heavens were made." The Hebrew word for *the presence of God* is the feminine *shekinah*. *Shekinah* accompanied the Hebrews through the desert as a pillar of fire and a cloud. In Exodus 16:10 the Hebrews "turned toward the desert, and lo, the glory of the LORD [*shekinah*] appeared in the cloud!"

Chokmah is a feminine word meaning "wisdom and understanding." Proverbs 3:19 tells us that God founded the earth by *chokmah* and set the heavens in place by *chokmah*. A voice from heaven that speaks God's will or judgment is the feminine *bat kol*. This word is used at Jesus' baptism when a dove comes down upon Him and He hears *bat kol*—a voice (Matthew 3:16–17) saying that God is pleased with Him.

Other Sources of Feminine Images

Church leaders and mystics have spoken of the feminine side of God. For example, a fifth-century bishop wrote of God, "You are father, you are mother, you are male, you are female." And a twelfth-century homilist helped people to understand how near God is by writing, "God is like a woman nursing the soul at her breasts, drying its tears, punishing its petty mischief-making, giving birth to it in agony and travail." Julian of Norwich, a fourteenth-century English mystic, wrote, "To the property of motherhood belong love, wisdom, and knowledge—and this is God."

In a talk delivered on September 10, 1978, Pope John Paul I cited Isaiah's question, "Can a mother forget her own child? But even if it should happen, God will never forget his people." The pope continued:

> We are the objects of undying love on the part of God. We know: God's eyes are always open to us, even when it seems to be dark. God is our father: even more God is our mother. God does not want to hurt us. God wants only to do good to us, to all of us. If children are ill, they have additional claims to be loved by their mother. And we too, if by chance we are sick with badness, on the wrong track, have yet another claim to be loved by [God].

His successor, Pope John Paul II, wrote a pastoral letter entitled "On the Dignity and Vocation of Women" (August 15, 1988). He said:

> This characteristic of biblical language—its anthropomorphic way of speaking about God—points indirectly to the mystery of the eternal "generating" which belongs to the inner life of God. Nevertheless, in itself this "generating" has neither "masculine" nor "feminine" qualities. It is by nature totally divine. It is spiritual in the most perfect way, since "God is spirit" (John 4:24) and possesses no property typical of the body, neither "feminine" nor "masculine." Thus even "fatherhood" in God is completely divine and free of the "masculine" bodily characteristics proper to human fatherhood.

So we have some history of feminine images, and current popes are reinforcing it. Yet, hearing God addressed as "Our

Father, Our Mother" startles and often angers people. How dare we address God as if God were female!

The intensity of people's responses to a change in words and images for God confirms the power of images. A change does bring about a different relationship with God and with other persons.

Prayer Changes If Our Images of God Change

How does a masculine or a feminine image of God affect the way a person prays? The image actually *pre-decides* how someone will relate to God. This is because both masculine and feminine set up certain expectations and call up certain responses.

Cultural tradition calls some personality traits masculine. Being competitive, assertive, protective, and logical are generally among them. Being nurturing, caring, understanding, and intuitive are usually described as feminine. Of course, everyone knows women with the so-called masculine traits and men with the so-called feminine ones. Most people have some of both qualities. Yet the perception of some qualities as masculine and some as feminine leads people to expect them in their "appropriate" sex.

Most people expect a different kind of interaction with a man in a position of authority than they do with a woman in that same position. In family, work, social occasions and academic settings, people meet each other with emotional expectations that are affected by whether they are meeting a man or a woman. They express surprise and often comment when a man shows predominantly feminine traits or a woman predominantly masculine ones.

So if people expect something different of men and women, what happens when they approach God in prayer as masculine? Inevitably such a pray-er will come to God with the same expectations and responses he or she would bring to an interaction with a man. In this process the feminine side of God is barely acknowledged.

Praying to a God Without Gender

Most people know God is spirit, and many say they don't picture God as man or woman when they pray. They experience God instead as light, wind, warmth, breath, or an embracing love.

Thinking about God with a neutral image is fairly easy. But I question whether many people are able to *relate emotionally* to a genderless being. Whenever people express love or praise in prayer, or seek solace or help, I believe they usually have some sense of a person to whom they are relating. Every person we know is either male or female.

So when people tell me that they have neither a masculine nor a feminine sense of God, I ask if they are equally comfortable with either pronoun for God. People relating to a genderless God will feel equally comfortable (or equally uncomfortable) with She or He. If hearing of God spoken about as "Him" causes no uneasiness while hearing "Her" does, then that person's *emotional* sense of God is probably masculine even though the visual image is not.

Is Expanding Our Images Worth the Effort?

Expanding our images of God is difficult. Yet any spiritual teacher will say that growth in relationship with God depends on regularly changing and expanding our images. Although prayer is harder during a transition time, a person's relationship with God is always fuller and more mature when a new image is integrated.

Dan, an engineer, told me that his picture of God and his prayer first changed when he shed a "punishing judge" image, which he recognized as he dealt with his feelings toward his overly strict father. But all his new images of a tender, caring God were challenged when his first wife died of cancer shortly after their second anniversary. God was not a judge, but neither did God "care enough" to protect him or his wife from suffering and pain.

Then Dan experienced a God to be wondered at as he watched his first child born to his second wife five years later. Each time Dan's image of God expanded, he found prayer difficult. But as he grew with the image, his relationship with God became better and deeper.

Judy, a young mother, had grown up with a fear of being punished by God. In her teens she rebelled, left home to live with a boyfriend, became pregnant, and gave birth to a child whom she parents alone. She gave up God and church altogether. Last year a friend invited her to a retreat weekend. She was afraid. But something in her wanted to go. During the two days she heard in a fresh way of a God who wanted her to receive love, of a God who cared personally about her, who forgave her and wanted to give her new hope and life.

As Judy's image of God evolved, her life slowly came together in a new way. She became more loving and open with her 8-year-old daughter. She started taking time for a few minutes of centering prayer each day. She began reading a scripture quotation each night before going to sleep. She felt more at ease and less alone.

Like Dan and Judy, our images of God must grow and expand if we are to grow and mature in relationship to God. In Judy's case, her life also changed as her image of God evolved.

What Our Images Convey

Joey had a rather clear image of God when he was 7. After church his parents, his 12-year-old sister, and he were riding in the car. They argued about where they would stop for lunch—McDonald's or Kentucky Fried Chicken. Joey blurted out, "Boys are better than girls, so I get to choose."

"Why do you say that, Joey?" his dad asked.

"Because God is a boy. I saw a picture of God, and he has a beard. So he must be a boy. God is better than anybody. So boys are better."

From thinking of God as a "boy" or as a man from early on, males take on a positive image of themselves as like God in a particular way, the way of their gender. Women grow up without this identification and the confidence and security it can give. In groups where women pray regularly with feminine images, they gradually become comfortable relating to God as a woman. I have witnessed many experiencing joyful peace as they came to realize that they flow from God as Her daughter. They come to know that they are a reflection of Her image. They are profoundly moved. They gain a new sense of themselves and their worth.

The Inferior Image of the Feminine

"Isn't Mary good enough for you?" a man shot angrily at some women who were listening enthusiastically to my words about imaging God as feminine. He seemed to be saying, "Must you also see yourself in the image of God? How arrogant!" Yet he didn't realize that he had so absorbed his own identification with God as male that he didn't even realize it. He identified himself with God and women with Mary. Mary, of course, was submissive to God—and as his subsequent remarks revealed submission was the heart of the issue.

Some men have a hard time accepting their own healthy feminine qualities. They've grown up with phrases like "Women are the weaker sex," or "Don't act like a sissy!"—meaning "like a girl." But if men's masculine qualities of protectiveness, aggressiveness, and competitiveness aren't balanced with the feminine qualities of nurturance, care, and emphasis on the importance of relationship, the male leadership of the world could obliterate the human race and destroy the earth. Masculine must be balanced with feminine if the earth is to continue to exist and the world to achieve peace.

Thinking of God as feminine could give men greater respect for women and what they can bring to the political world, and it might become easier for them to trust and accept the feminine in themselves.

The God of Our Child Within

Psychologists tell us that children *feel* that God the Father is like their own fathers—no matter what visual image is taught or shown to them. Those who can trust their fathers to fill their needs will also trust God. Those who fear their father's criticism and punishments will also fear God's. Those who are abused—physically, psychologically, or sexually—may keep an emotional distance from God.

Children usually carry their early feelings about God into adulthood—even if their images change or their knowledge contradicts those feelings. If those who have had untrustworthy, absentee, authoritarian, critical, or abusive fathers want to experience God's loving care for them, they have several choices. They can, for example, prayerfully cultivate the image of the father they longed to have. They can then fill their hearts and imaginations with this picture, knowing that God has all the characteristics of

32   CALLED INTO HER PRESENCE

their ideal father. In this way the image of God the Father can be
healing.

Or they can turn to God the Mother—or Sister—or Friend—
and connect with that God the good things they have experienced
in one of these relationships. Praying with She and Her can then
shatter a negative male image of God and free the pray-er for love
and trust.

When someone's experience of his or her mother is negative, the Mother-God image can call up fear, anxiety, or anger.
This person can understandably stay with the Father-image or
male God—or move toward healing within by picturing the ideal
mother and knowing that her qualities are God's.

Does Mary Image the Feminine of God?

Some Catholics tell me that Mary has always supplied their
faith with a special feminine image and that they find themselves
picturing Mary as they begin to pray with a feminine image of
God. Others complain with some anger that a feminine image of
God displaces Mary who, they say, is *the* image of mother given
to us by God.

The *image* of Mary, which has inspired so much devotion that
some has even turned into worship, has also sparked ambivalent
feelings in many women. Some experience her as a close friend
and companion. Others have difficulty relating to her because
she seems above ordinary women—someone on an unattainable
pedestal. Some give up on her as a model, complaining that a
woman who is both virgin and mother is impossible to emulate.
Others believe she has been used—destructively—to reinforce the
submission of women to men.

Mary, more than any other woman, reflects for us the feminine side of God. The key word is *reflects*. Although some devo-
tions and traditions down through the centuries have put Mary
above women—and some would say, have made a goddess of
her—in the Hail Mary we call Mary blessed *among* women. Gab-
riel, the messenger of God, told Mary that of all women in the
world she is the most fortunate, the most blessed by God. As
a woman *among* us, Mary is easier to befriend, less difficult to

imagine as a person who lived—and perhaps struggled with—faith, hope, and love. Mary is first among us, the disciples of Jesus.

Perhaps people raised Mary so high above to compensate for centuries of denial of the feminine of God. Worshiping God as God, both feminine and masculine, can help many women and men rediscover Mary as one of us, a human being who was a reflective person (Lk 2:51), an intelligent questioner of God (Lk 1:34), an advocate of social justice (Lk 1:51–53), a person who sought in faith to do the will of God (Lk 1:38), and who was more even blessed for this than for being the mother of the Son of God (Mk 3:34–35). We can see her as a woman who didn't despair even under the worst of sufferings, watching the torturous death of her son (Jn 19:25).

The Need for Many Images

God is beyond all that we can know. We seek those qualities, those images of God for which we have the greatest need at any one time of our lives. As children, we may have needed a Santa Claus image of God, the belief that God will let only good things happen to us if we are good, that we will be punished if we are bad. Children are seldom ready for the injustice that characterizes life. (That is not to say that we are ready as adults either.)

As we face crises and tragedies and try to survive what seem to be impossible situations and circumstances, "It's not fair" comes to our lips. That image of God as showering blessings on the good and punishments on the evil in this life is inadequate. We search for who God is and how God is present in our lives. We look for the images that will integrate us or comfort us or express our insights.

Laura, for instance, is only 19. She tells me she needs a father-image of God right now to replace her father who died last year. David, a teenager, says he needs a mother image since his parents separated last year and he is with his father. Julie finds women easier to talk to; seeing God as a feminine friend makes prayer so much easier. Al feels a need to go "straight to headquarters" with a request and senses that, in this case, a dominant male image of God is appropriate for him.

Expanding Images in Communal Worship

Each person has an individual image of God in keeping with his or her individual relationship to God. No two images or relationships are alike. Yet people also have a communal image of God. This picture of God is handed down to us in our communities, which interpret (theologize) their experiences of God or those of their ancestors. We recognize and celebrate our collective images when we worship together.

We need collective images of God or we could never come together and pray. So we use *Father* even though we know that we have many individual images for God called up by that word. We celebrate God as *Lord* of all of creation. In the Eucharist we become aware of God's presence within ourselves and each other. We sign the cross and give blessings because of our common belief in the mystery of a Triune God.

Although different nationalities and ethnic groups use the same words and images, they interpret them differently. If the way people express themselves in worship is any indication of the way they see God and their relationship with God, then the words *Father* and *Lord* have vastly different meanings—even in the Catholic tradition—to Mexicans, West Germans, Jamaicans, the Polish of Milwaukee, the Irish of Boston, African Americans, and Native Americans. Just watch their celebrations for evidence of this.

Consider further how the words *father* or *lord* or *king* or *suffering servant* inspired different relationships and religious expressions to the early Jewish Christians and Gentile Christians, to people of the Middle Ages, to those who experienced European royalty and titles, to those under the spell of Francis of Assisi or the French Jansenists. Those who identify with Thomistic theology (influenced by Aristotle and other Greek philosophers) experience their relationship with God differently from those who are influenced by Bernard Lonergan or process theologians or twentieth-century findings in psychology or physics.

Despite the differences, we who call ourselves Christian are able to find common words and images in order to pray together. We find common words and images to share prayer with our sisters and brothers of all faiths. We all accept some communal images, even though our variations on that image are as great as the number of people praying together.

When we pray privately, we can choose any images and words we wish. The imagery of private prayer is not easy to change, but we can do this fairly quickly compared to the time needed to change communal prayer. It is the communal images, however, that shape the children and new community members and influence our religious, political, and social structures.

If we care about justice, we need to begin working to expand our public images of God. If we care for our own sanity, we need to realize that communal change takes a long time. Many individuals need to embrace new images first in their private prayer or small-group prayer. Eventually those images will pervade our communal worship.

Six Reasons to Balance Our Masculine Images With Feminine Ones

In summary, I offer six reasons why all of us, both women and men, should enlarge our images of God to include the feminine:

- ◆ to know God better and to relate to God with a fuller sense of who God is;
- ◆ to help recognize that feminine qualities are as necessary for guiding the world as masculine ones;
- ◆ to help women identify with God as daughters in the way men already unconsciously feel the connection to God as sons;
- ◆ to help men and women reach wholeness by making it easier for them to embrace their feminine side;
- ◆ to provide an alternative for those who have difficulty relating to God as a father;
- ◆ to provide a feminine image of healing for those who have had less than adequate mothering.

I believe we live closer to the truth of God as we are able to live and pray comfortably with both masculine and feminine images of God.

"Faith begins not in the word and the concept, but in the image and the symbol," writes John Henry Cardinal Newman. As human beings, we shape our images and symbols of God. In turn, these images and symbols shape us. They become lenses for our faith, for our way of looking at ourselves, for our relationships to one another, our society, our economics, and our politics. Let us be aware of our choices in prayer. Then let us pray—asking for greater knowledge of God, and a fuller experience of God's love, which surpasses all knowledge, so that we "may be filled with all the fullness of God" (Eph 3:19).

PART TWO

*Praying With Feminine
Images of God:
Exercises, Experiences,
and Celebrations*

Loving Oneself in the Present Moment

Opening Prayer

My Mother and my God, I believe in your total, unconditional love for me. You embrace me, nurture me, teach and counsel me. Your forgiveness makes my healing possible.

I want to live in your love and the truth of your love for me. How can I love myself as you do? Keep me from expecting more of myself than you expect from me. Help me to learn from my mistakes, not condemn myself for making them. Help me to forgive myself when I have hurt others, when I have failed to live in love.

Deliver me from a super image of myself. Teach me to accept my limitations and not push my body beyond the strength you breathe into it. Show me how to balance the needs of others with my own needs. Help me to listen for your voice as I am deciding whether to say yes or no. Teach me. Counsel me.

GUIDED IMAGERY MEDITATION

Is there a more powerful feminine symbol than a womb? The Bible often ascribes pregnancy and birth to God.

I have looked away, and kept silence,
    I have said nothing, holding myself in;
But now, I cry out as a woman in labor (Is 42:14).

In [God] we live and move and have our being (Acts 17:28).

Salvation is shown as a birth process in Romans:

All creation is groaning in labor pains (Rom 8:22).

For this meditation imagine yourself in God's womb, being nurtured by Her as you both await your birth.

Breathe deeply several times. Become conscious of your breathing. Let it gently fill your body. Do this long enough to become relaxed and centered within yourself.

Begin your prayer by gazing at yourself as a mother gazes at her child, and as your Mother God beholds you. Gently accept yourself as you are now—at this age and at whatever place you are in your physical, spiritual, and psychological growth.

A mother affirms her child. To affirm means to recognize and accept in a loving way. With your Mother God, affirm yourself.

First, affirm your own appearance—your particular eyes, nose, mouth, ears, face, your arms, your legs, your upper body, your lower body, your femininity, your masculinity.

Identify the parts of your body that are most beautiful, most pleasing to you. Feel your Mother God enclosing you and those pleasing parts of your body with Her love also.

Identify the part or parts of your body that you find hard to accept. Feel the loving, encompassing womb of your Mother and your God infusing those parts with Her love.

Affirm your own breathing, your respiratory system as it takes in oxygen to your lungs and to all parts of your body, cleansing it, giving each cell new life.

Affirm your heart and your circulatory system, this center from which your physical life radiates, this system pumping nourishment through a complicated system of routes so intricately and perfectly connected.

Affirm your digestive system. Begin with your mouth and its ability to receive food with pleasure. Consider the marvelous complexity of the system through which the food travels and is changed into sources of energy for you.

Affirm your reproductive system—and the great power you have to co-create with God.

Affirm also your desire to care for your own body as your Mother God nurtures you and cares for you.

Affirm your own personality—the outgoing part of yourself and your inwardness. Affirm the way both are a part of you in your particular proportions. Recall some of your own personality characteristics. Are you forceful and truthful? Or gentle and understanding? Outgoing and generous in helping others? Are you able to commit yourself to some quiet solitary effort and stay with it? Do you appreciate a well-turned literary phrase or an exquisitely played piece of music? Can you get absorbed in cheering your favorite sports teams? What interests you most? When do you feel most alive? What makes you sad? What angers you? Think of any other personality traits *you* have. Affirm now your special personality as separate and different from all others. Feel yourself in the womb being cherished for who you are.

What gifts or skills do you bring to others?
Are you good with tools? Able to fix the plumbing?
Can you play a guitar—or another instrument? Tell
a joke well? Can you listen to another with quiet
acceptance? Do you have a good sense of humor? Or
what we call down-to-earth common sense? Perhaps
you can take care of a person who is ill or disabled
with respect and patience. Or can you cook? Relate to
children? Are you able to plan a party? Give gifts you
have made yourself? Service or repair a car? Tend a
garden?

Think about the particular gift or skills you offer.
Affirm them in yourself. Experience the embracing
affirmation of God as you use your gifts to enhance
life for yourself and for others.

In what ways are you developing in this womb
existence? How are you growing now? Are you
becoming more understanding and accepting of your
own self? Are you more open to others and able to
receive them with their faults? Remember, most of
us will never reach perfection in these things. Gently
growing in them is the important movement. Are you
growing mentally—continuing to learn something?
Are you open to new insights? Do you accept your
views of life being challenged? Are you growing less
judgmental? Less prejudiced?

In the suffering and difficulties and stress of
your life in this womb existence, are you growing
in compassion toward yourself and others? If your
womb existence of this life is filled with much
darkness, are you able to keep your eyes on the
distant light, even when it seems dim?

As you develop, are you growing in appreciating
the good things of each day? Seeing a raindrop on
a leaf? Hearing a cricket after sunset? Pushing your
fingers into the fur of a puppy? Are you aware and
appreciative of having food on your table? Of having
a place to sleep? Of someone's friendly hello? Of an
hour or two to do something you enjoy?

And are you growing—remember, the word is growing, not achieving—in hope and patience and humor as you cope with the ordinary distresses of daily life—a head cold, trouble with the car, a friend's misunderstanding of your words, a cup of coffee spilled on your clothing, the breakdown of an appliance?

Wherever you are in your development be at rest right now in your womb enclosure. Feel yourself relaxed in your Mother God's nurturing acceptance and love. Hear Her speak to you in the words of Isaiah:

> Can a mother forget her infant,
> be without tenderness for the child
> of her womb?
> Even should she forget,
> I will never forget you (Is 49:15).

As you exist right now, growing within the hollow of the womb, experience again the nurturing and unconditional love of God as She exalts in you at whatever point in your growth you may be, rejoices in you with whatever growth has happened so far, and awaits with warm eagerness your further development into the person you will be when She births you into eternity.

Feel the vibrant maternal power of the One who holds you within Her, fully aware of you, loving you with unending love, and waiting for the time to come when She will be able to embrace you in fullness.

Rest in Her. Receive Her love.

Reflection/Discussion Starters

What does it mean to *affirm* someone? To affirm yourself?

What parts of your body did you find it easy to affirm? What parts were difficult to affirm?

Was it easier to identify the parts you consider beautiful or the parts you find hard to accept?

What did you experience in affirming your respiratory, circulatory, digestive, and reproductive systems?

What personality characteristics could you affirm? What gifts or skills?

Do you believe that God affirms you at *this* moment, wherever you are in your growth?

What feelings were evoked in you by the experience of being enclosed in the womb of God? By waiting to be embraced by God as Mother?

Scripture: Romans 8:22 (all creation is groaning); and Isaiah 49:15 (can a mother forget?).

FOR PERSONAL PRAYER

Her Faithfulness

1) Open your bible to Isaiah 49:15. Set it aside.

2) Breathe slowly several times, becoming conscious of each breath as you inhale and exhale. Feel it traveling through your body. Continue this until you feel your body relaxing.

3) Take several more breaths and be aware of God's Spirit filling you each time you inhale. God's power is re-creating you at this moment.

4) Read Isaiah 49:15. Hear Her say these words to you. Hear Her put your name in the promise: "I will never forget you, ———." Keep rereading the passage, hearing the words spoken to you over and over again.

5) Respond to Her promise of faithful love.

My Faithfulness

1) Find a place where you will not be interrupted.

2) Focus on some parts of your body—each for a minute or two; for example, look at a finger, the palm of your hand, your knee; feel the pulse of your heartbeat in your left foot, the vibrations in a toe.

3) Be aware of your whole body. Feel yourself centered in it.

4) Become conscious of Her presence deep within you or all around you.

5) In Her presence, ask yourself the following questions:

Do I *know* that I am loved by God?

In what ways has She shown me love?

Do I *feel* that I am unconditionally loved by Her?

What obstacles keep me from receiving Her love and living in it?

6) Speak with Her about these things.

7) Listen.

Psalm Parallel (Psalm 139)

Mother, you have given me birth
    and cared for me ever since;
You are familiar with all my ways.
You know all that I do, to whom I speak;
You even know what I am thinking.
Before a word jumps onto my tongue,
My God, you seem to know it.
You know my whole journey,
    Every thicket and resting place along my path.
You walk in front of me and behind me;
Sometimes I feel your hand resting on my shoulder.
This faithfulness of your loving presence
Seems too good to be true.

Could I go away from you—or your spirit?
Is any place locked from your presence?
If I fly to the heavens, won't you be there?
If I sink to the depths of the earth,
     I think I would meet you still.
If I flew on the wings of the dawn,
If I sailed to the far limits of the sea,
Your hand would still be upon me
Guiding me, holding me safe.

You formed me before I was born.
You have created my inner self.
Thank you for making me so wonderful!
     (All your works are wonderful!)
You always understand my spirit;
You know each cell of my body.
You have been with me in all that I have done
And will be with me until the end.
Your plan is wonderful, more than I can grasp;
I rest in you in faith and live in you in love.

PERSONAL RITUAL

Choose a quality about yourself that you accept with love. Tell an understanding family member or friend about it and how you use it, or can use it, to enhance your life and the lives of others.

COMMON RITUAL

Preparation

For each participant cut out a circle made from tracing a dinner plate on plain paper. Make a few extra ones.
Have colored chalk and/or colored pencils ready.

Place a feminine symbol for God on a small round table. (The symbol could be a round vase, a bowl, an egg—perhaps decorated, a round loaf of bread, and so on.) Position a chair for each participant in a circle around the table.

When all are seated, show the group one of the circles and explain that it is a *mandala*. A mandala is a circle, and it represents wholeness. Mandalas are common in art; for example, rose windows, circles with symbols in them in churches, decorative plates, ornate round shields. Give each person a circle and say something like this:

> You each have a circle—and they are quite similar to one another. To turn your circle into a mandala, give it colors or symbols or pictures that represent you *at this moment*. Fortunately, no one needs to be an artist in order to make a mandala.
>
> You might consider how you feel at this moment or this point of your life and choose some colors to represent these feelings or this place in which you find yourself. Let the colors flow and the lines take shape as they come to you. Or draw a symbolic picture, for example, a door to represent new beginnings, a web to show present struggles, or a flower to say life has come to a full bloom.
>
> You will have fifteen or twenty minutes to do this. I suggest that you find a private place where you can ponder first and then make your mandala. I have extra circles in case anyone wants to begin again.
>
> When you return, we will invite you to share the meaning or part of the meaning of your mandalas, but only to the extent that you feel comfortable. No one has to share anything.

Ritual

One member opens with a spontaneous prayer and, if necessary, explains the meaning of the central symbol on the "altar."

All sing "Mother and God" from *WomanSong* by Miriam Therese Winter, or "Rahamin" from *Cry of Ramah* by Colleen Fulmer (see Appendix B).

One member begins the sharing by holding up his or her mandala and praying with these or similar words:

> Mother, as you love me, so, with your grace, I intend to love myself. I bring this mandala to symbolize _____. I offer it to You. (Or, for those who do not wish to share the meaning of their mandalas, "I bring this mandala, and I offer it to You.")

As the person places the mandala on the altar, the group responds,

> We affirm you and offer your mandala to our Mother and our God with you.

All sing "Blessing Song" from *Womansong* by Miriam Therese Winter, or "A Blessing Song" from *Circling Free* by Marsie Silvestro (see Appendix B).

Trust in Her

Opening Prayer

God, you want me to trust in you. As I sit in the sunlight of your word, I do. Sometimes, however, clouds settle in and rain begins to fall. I cannot see in front of myself. I give in to worry and fear. I find it hard to feel your presence in pelting hail and chilling winds. I cry out to you. I believe that you are there. When the sunlit skies reappear, I find trust easy and promise I will not so easily fall into anxiety and excessive fear again. I am weak. I need you even to help me trust you.

GUIDED IMAGERY MEDITATION

Before you begin, a little background on this theme may prove helpful. In various places the biblical writers enlist the eagle as a metaphor for God. Because the female eagle of biblical lands was the larger and stronger of a pair, and except for a short time after the birth of the eaglets, she did more of the hunting for food, some scholars believe that the writers based their metaphors on the female bird. Evidence of this exists in earlier biblical texts—down to and including the *King James Version*—which use feminine pronouns in the passages.

Now, as you begin this meditation, ask God for some particular gift, something which She can give you within this ten or fifteen minutes of prayer. Make it something that will enable you to say at the end of this meditation, "Yes, I received it." Or "No, She did not give it to me." Your request may be for the ability to pray during this time or for a sense of Her presence or for an insight into yourself or into Her. Ask for the gift *you* want to receive during *this* prayer time.

Begin this prayer by relaxing all your muscles. Then imagine that you see an eagle perched in her nest on a cliff. Look at her full and majestic contours, her colors, and the colors of the earth and rock around her. Overhead is a clear blue sky. The eagle is moving now, standing, and lifting her wings. She is preparing to take off. She lifts herself up and out into the air. Watch her strong and sure gliding movements. She is soaring into the sky, carving a path through it. Watch her sweep a curve. As you follow her movements, recall that biblical writers said that God is like an eagle. What do the following quotations about eagles reveal of God to us?

From the *King James Version* of Deuteronomy 32:11–12:

> As an eagle stirreth up her nest, fluttereth over her young, spreadeth abroad her wings, taketh them, beareth them on her wings:
>   so the LORD alone did lead [Jacob].

Chapter 12 of the Book of Revelation tells us that the woman gave birth to the divine child, who was snatched up to heaven for safety, and then [the woman] was given the "wings of the great eagle, so that she could fly to her place in the desert" (Rv 12:14).

Isaiah writes:

> They that hope in the LORD will renew
> their strength,
> they will soar as with eagles' wings;
> They will run and not grow weary,
> walk and not grow faint (Is 40:31).

For a few minutes, let yourself be an eaglet in the following myth about how eagles teach their young to fly:

Feel yourself secure within the shelter of a nest. Although high on a mountain cliff, you are safe in this nest, which has been woven for you. You are fed and you are shielded from the sight of any enemies. Your parents' large wings cover you at the slightest danger.

You grow. And a time comes when you must learn to fly, to find food for yourself. Your mother bears you out of the nest, mounted on her back. She flies while you enjoy the ride. Now she swoops down and out, separating herself from you and leaving you free to try your own wings. Yet she is sweeping down under you and is ready to catch you in case you should fall. Your mother has led you to this new experience, but she will not let you fall to your destruction. She is eager for you to find your own strength, your own maturity. She wants you, someday, to be strong and equal in flight to herself. Feel her bearing you up, giving you strength, then letting *you* fly again, as she deftly positions herself below you, providing the safety you need.

Pray this paraphrase of a psalm written thousands of years ago. Speak these words to your own heart and to others you know who put their trust in God.

You who dwell in the shelter of the Most High,
    who live in the shadow of the Almighty,
Say to your God: You are my refuge and my
    stronghold,
My God in whom I trust.
For She will rescue you from those who will trap
    you,
        from any evil which destroys.
Under Her wings She will hold you, and under
    Her wings you shall find safety.
Her faithfulness is a shield of defense.
You need not fear the terror of night
Nor the arrows that fly by day.
For to Her angels She has given Her commands,
That they guard you in all that you do.
Upon their hands they shall bear you up,
Lest you dash your foot against a stone.

And now, hear your female-eagle-God say to you in these paraphrased words of Psalm 91:

Because you love me, I will rescue you.
I will protect you because you acknowledge me.
You shall call upon me, and I will answer you;
I will be with you in distress.
I will deliver you and honor you and save you.

Soar awhile with your eagle-God. Be *free*, yet aware of Her protective watching. Soar as long as you like.

Before you close your prayer, recall the request you made for a gift during this prayer time. Speak to God about whether or not She granted it.

Option: You may want to close the meditation with the song "Great Soaring Spirit" from *Bring Many Names* by Brian Wren (see Appendix B).

Reflection/Discussion Starters

Describe the eagle and her nest as you pictured them.

How did you feel as you watched the eagle take off and soar?

What did you experience when you were in the nest? As you set out being carried by your mother eagle? As she separated herself from you? As you realized she was below you?

What did your eagle-mother want for you?

Could you experience the eagle as female? How is this image appropriate for God?

Scripture: Deuteronomy 32:11–12 (the eagle stirs her nest); Exodus 19:4 (I bore you on eagle's wings); Revelation 12:14 (woman given wings of eagle); Isaiah 40:31 (they will soar with eagle's wings); and adaptation of Psalm 91.

For Personal Prayer

Choose one of the following prayer exercises. Find a quiet place and relax until you feel calm. Then use your imagination to enter into one of the following prayers:

The God of Life's Bridges

Your God asks you to meet Her on a bridge. Go to a bridge of your choice and walk out to the middle of it. You will find Her there. Greet Her.

She looks at you, says your name, and asks you if you trust Her. Answer Her.

"I shall always be with you."

Hear Her, your God, say to you over and over:

> With you I will be close;
> you have hold of my hand (paraphrase of Ps 73:23).

Respond with:

> How good it is to be near God
> to make Her my refuge (paraphrase of Ps 73:28).

Resting as a Child

Pray the following paraphrase of Psalm 131:1–2 over and over again, both silently and aloud. Rest in Her.

> O God, my heart is not proud,
> nor are my eyes haughty;
> I busy not myself with great things,
> nor with things too sublime for me.
> Nay rather, I have stilled and quieted
> my soul like a weaned child;
> Like a weaned child on its mother's lap,
> (so is my soul within me).

I rest in you my God.

Praying a Mantra

A mantra is a breath prayer that uses seven syllables. Breathe in on the first three syllables and breathe out on the last three. The middle syllable is the breath change between breathing in and breathing out. Praying a mantra is made easier by closing your eyes or focusing on an empty space, a candle flame, a rock, or some simple, single object.

Pray one of the mantras suggested below for three to five minutes. Let your sense of God be that of God's feminine presence. Let any distractions fade away—into space or the flame or the air around you. Continue to pray the mantra each day—increasing the time by a minute or two—until you can pray this way for ten to twenty minutes.

> *These mantras reflect God speaking to you:*
> With you I shall always be.
> You are made in my image.
> My love shall never leave you.
> I will never forget you.
> Come, and I will refresh you.
> Who do you say that I am?

These mantras reflect you speaking to God:
>Your love is everlasting.
>
>My Sister (or Mother or caring) God, you I trust.
>
>With you I shall always be.
>
>I trust in your love for me.
>
>In your wings I find refuge.

Psalm Parallel (Psalm 57)

Hear my prayers, my God; hear my prayers
for you are my shelter from this storm.
In the shadow of your wings I am protected.
Keep me from any more harm.

I call to God in my fear,
to Her who has always given good gifts.
May She come to save me;
May Her spirit within me conquer my foes;
May She show me Her kindness and faithfulness.

I lie down in the midst of anxiety;
I get up with worry encompassing me.
Their teeth are knives in my spirit;
Their feet trample my soul.

You are a tower of strength,
I need to cling to you.

I speak to my family—
They do not understand.
I turn to my friends—
Wonder is in their eyes.
But you, my God, hear me and know me
And offer your strength to lift up mine.

Awake!
Get up, my soul, and sing Her praises.
She takes the dread out of the night,

She rises with me at dawn.
I give thanks for Her kindness and faithfulness.
Praise Her, everyone!

PERSONAL RITUAL

Write down one fear or anxiety you experience. Place it in a bowl or plant or shell or other feminine symbol of your God. When the worry or fear returns, go to the symbol, place your hand upon it, and give the anxiety back to Her.

If you are fortunate enough to carry few fears or anxieties, praise Her for this gift by writing a line or two, or drawing a picture and placing it in a feminine symbol of God.

COMMON RITUAL

Preparation

Write the scripture quotations about trust (that appear at the end of this chapter) on separate slips of paper, or on meaningful symbolic shapes such as fish, cocoons, lilies, birds, rosebuds. Place them all in a beautiful bowl and set it on a small round table in the center of a circle of chairs.

Ask a reader to prepare Matthew 6:26–34, substituting either "God" or "Father/Mother" for the word *Father*, which appears twice.

Ritual

All sing "Mystery" from *WomanSong* by Miriam Therese Winter, or "Rahamin" (with gestures) from *Cry of Ramah* by Colleen Fulmer, or "Ruah" from *Cry of Ramah* by Colleen Fulmer (see Appendix B). Or you may play the tape for the verses and ask all to sing the chorus.

Reading: Matthew 6:26–34.

Ask for statements—or statements of questions ("I am wondering why...")—that flow from the reading. Receive each contribution, but do not discuss any of them. Eye contact or a simple thank you is enough.

Tell the group about the contents of the bowl in the center. Direct participants to follow one of the following options.

Option 1: A volunteer comes forward, takes a quotation from the bowl, and reads it aloud. Follow with a minute of silence. (You may wish to time the sixty seconds on your watch since it is difficult to judge.) Another volunteer does the same, and a minute of silence follows. Continue until all the quotations are read.

Option 2: Be sure that one quotation is in the bowl for each person. Ask everyone to come forward and take one. Ask each person to leave the circle and illustrate in some way the quotation he or she received—draw a picture, sketch a mandala, prepare to tell a story (fact or fiction), cut a picture from a magazine, do a mime. If the group is large, several people can work together on one quotation. Skits, commercials, and dialogues then become possible.

Each person (or group) returns for a presentation. Set an example of vigorous applause or some other positive response to each contribution.

Call the group to a few minutes of silence to reflect on what they have learned or better understood or what they have felt called to during this time of reflection. Invite brief spontaneous prayers.

Close with the song "You, God, Are My Firmament" or "Blessed Is She" from *WomanSong* by Miriam Therese Winter. Or read "Rest in My Wings" and sing "Mantle of Light" from *Cry of Ramah* by Colleen Fulmer (see Appendix B).

Quotations for the Common Ritual:

Even to your old age I am the same,
  even when your hair is gray I will bear you;
It is I who have done this, I who will continue,
  and I who will carry you to safety (Is 46:4).

Though the mountains leave their place
  and the hills be shaken,

My love shall never leave you
    nor my covenant of peace be shaken,
    says the LORD, who has mercy on
        you (Is 54:10).

All you who are thirsty,
    come to the water!
You who have no money,
    come, receive grain and eat (Is 55:1).

. . . I have stilled and quieted
    my soul like a weaned child.
Like a weaned child on its mother's lap,
    [so is my soul within me] (Ps 131).

God is my shepherdess, all my needs
        are met,
She gives me rest
        in green pastures (paraphrase of Ps 23).

Only in God is my soul at rest;
    in Her I find my salvation,
    . . . I will not be defeated.
She is my shield and shelter (paraphrase of Ps 62).

Fear not, for I have redeemed you;
    I have called you by name: you are mine.
When you pass through the water, I
        will be with you;
    in the rivers you shall not drown.
When you walk through fire, you shall
        not be burned;
    the flames shall not consume you (Is 43:1–2).

For you have said, "My kindness is
        established forever";
    in heaven you have confirmed your
        faithfulness (Ps 89:3).

Can a mother forget her infant,
    be without tenderness for the child
        of her womb?
Even should she forget,
    I will never forget you (Is 49:15).

And behold, I am with you always, until the end of the age (Mt 28:20).

Ask and it will be given to you (Mt 7:7).

Seek and you will find (Mt 7:7).

Knock and the door will be opened to you (Mt 7:7).

For everyone who asks, receives; and the one who seeks, finds; and to the one who knocks, the door will be opened (Mt 7:8).

As bad as you are, you know how to give good things to your children. How much more, then, will your Mother/Father in heaven give good things to those who ask (paraphrase of Mt 7:11).

All you ask...in my name God will give you (paraphrase of Jn 15:16).

Receiving Her Forgiveness

Opening Prayer

God, Jesus says you are like a homemaker, like a woman who loses something valuable and then drops everything to go in search of it. You have often come in search of me. Help me to value myself with the value you place on me.

I slip from your arms, forget your love and get lost in my desires for things that will not last. When you reach out and bring me back again, I expect you to be hard on me as I am often hard on myself. Yet you are not. You rejoice in having me back. Your kind of love and forgiveness are hard to believe. You are a wonder, my God.

GUIDED IMAGERY MEDITATION

Three parables in chapter 15 of Luke's gospel dramatize God's great love, forgiveness, and mercy. One presents God as a forgiving father who welcomes home his erring son. In another the image of God is

a shepherd who goes in search of one sheep that is
lost. In the third God is pictured as a woman who
searches for a lost coin in her home. In the following
guided meditation, we will ponder this homemaker
image of God.

To prepare yourself to enter into this prayer, find
a comfortable position, one in which you are both
alert and relaxed. If you are sitting in a chair, it is
helpful to place both feet on the floor and to keep
your back straight. If you are lying down, do not use
a pillow. Lie straight and flat on your back.

Feel your body in contact with the floor or chair
or bed. Feel the hardness or softness of the surfaces.
Feel heavy against them.

Breathe in a deep, slow breath and let it out
slowly. Breathe in again a bit more deeply, yet
without forcing your breath. Do this several times.
Breathe until you are relaxed. Feel your body again
on the surfaces on which you are resting. Breathe
in once more and, as you exhale, picture the gospel
scene of a woman looking for a lost coin in her home.

What woman having ten coins and losing one
would not light a lamp and sweep the house,
searching carefully until she finds it? (Lk 15:8).

Look at her sweeping, bending from the waist
to see if she can catch a gleam of something shining.
Watch her get down on her knees to search the floor.
Can you see the tension and anxiety of her body
as she searches? Just now she is catching a sliver of
reflected light to her left. Watch her quick movement
toward it and see her pick up the coin. She brushes it
against her clothing, looks at it, and holds it tightly.
Can you sense her relief and joy?

Can you think of a time—or several times—
when you have lost something valuable? If you can't
remember a specific thing, can you recall what it feels
like to discover you have lost something? How do
you feel? What do you do? Do you ask for help or try

to find it yourself? Do you panic or stay calm? Can you remember the joy—and the relief—of finding what you lost?

In the parable about the woman who lost the coin, Jesus is telling us that God searches for us, for whatever may be hidden or lost in us, with as much desire to find us as the woman's desire to find the coin. God's desire to find you is even greater than the desire with which you have searched for what is valuable to you.

And Jesus tells us that all of heaven rejoices with God when She finds us. Like that coin, we too may be powerless about being lost, aware that we cannot find ourselves or some lost parts of ourselves just by our own efforts. Precisely in our weakness, God wants to find us, clasp us to Herself, and bring us to greater wholeness, bring us to oneness with Her.

To bring this gospel truth to life, think of some part of yourself that seems lost. It may be a hidden part—or an obvious part of yourself—that needs to be found, to be healed, to be liberated or integrated.

Is some part of you lost, for instance, in an inability to forgive someone? Or in not being able to forgive yourself? Or lost in the habit of making judgments about others? Or lost to your uncontrollable temper? Or to a constant drive for financial gain—or to constant worry about money? Is, perhaps, a part of you lost in an addiction to overeating or to caffeine or tobacco or alcohol? Or to a habit of gossiping? Or sarcasm? Or put-downs?

Are you lacking in compassion, unwilling to reach out to someone who needs listening or visiting or understanding? Could you be lost in apathy toward social injustices?

Are you lost in an inability to give your body respect and what you need physically—rest or balanced meals or sleep or exercise or times of leisure?

Are some of your talents lost because you are afraid to use them? Are you afraid to fail?

Could you be lost in overwork or self-pity? In withdrawing to protect yourself? Or in worrying?

If you can, identify with one of these ways of being lost—or another way of your own not mentioned.

Let yourself center in that lost part for a few moments. How do you feel (weak, separate, broken, wounded) as you try to respond to the gospel message from this center? For these few moments, feel yourself alone, aware of your weakness—and wait.

God hears you name the lost or wounded part of yourself. She, your God, has always loved you—always held you invisibly in Her embrace and ached whenever you pulled away from Her. She has loved you in your weakness and longed to heal you. She hears you now and is coming in search of you. Watch Her from a distance and see Her concern for you, Her desire to find you, heal you, release you, to touch you into feeling whole and alive and in communion with yourself and other people and Her.

Observe Her searching for you, looking everywhere, and slowly making Her way to you with love and care. She is searching for *you*. Yet, She limits Her own power. She will not invade you, not find you against your will. You must want Her to find you. She is coming closer. And closer. How do you feel as She gets near? Can you make yourself visible to Her?

Let Her find you. Let Her discover the lost part of yourself and reach out to you. Feel Her taking hold of you with a joyful, loving, and healing embrace. And know also the joy of others—Her friends—your friends—for there is more joy over one repentant person, over one lost person who is found, than over ninety-nine who have no need to change their lives.

Let Her welcome you as a lost one and rejoice in you. She has taken you into Her arms. Remain as long as you wish in Her loving embrace and respond to Her in any way that is comfortable to you.

Reflection/Discussion Starters

Describe your picture of the woman looking for the lost coin; for example, the kind of clothing, house, room, furniture, her facial expression.

How do you feel when you lose something valuable? What is the first thing you do? What else do you do?

What object(s) of value have you lost? Did you find it (them)? If you did, how did you respond?

What part of yourself did you identify as lost or in need of freedom or healing? What did it feel like to center yourself in this weak or lost part?

Do you believe that God wants to free you? Heal you?

What were your feelings as a female-homemaker-God came in search of you—the lost coin? Is it easier or harder to imagine this event than to have a male-shepherd-God in search of you—the lost sheep?

Describe your experience of being found.

Scripture: Luke 15:8–10 *(parable of the lost coin).*

FOR PERSONAL PRAYER

Release to Prisoners (based on Isaiah 61:1)

Imagine youself in a place that is ugly and confining. Acknowledge that you do not like to be here. Notice everything around you. Touch the walls and any objects you see. What do you hear? Do you smell any odors?

What *part* of you does this room represent? Are the walls made of *fear*—confining you? Are they a *compulsion* that binds you? A place of *unforgiven hurts, slights and betrayals?* A vault of *pride?* A den of *self-hatred?*

Name what it is that confines you and surrounds you. Can you forgive yourself for whatever holds you in this place? Or accept yourself? Take time to consider this and, if you are not able to forgive and accept yourself, pray to be able to do so.

Can you reach out to touch this place again, but touch it with forgiveness—and even love?

The place is filling with light, a soft and glowing light. This light is surrounding you and penetrating you. Feel it reaching every part of your body. From within the light, hear Her, your God, say: "I am with you. I love you. I forgive you. I will be your strength."

Read Isaiah 61:1.

Help for Your Journey

Choose three different places for this prayer, for example, three spots outdoors, three rooms in a house, three chairs. If you can't move around for this prayer, choose three places in your imagination.

Name some difficulty you experience such as losing your temper; being a perfectionist; not being able to show love; continual overindulgence in food, drink, work, or leisure.

Go to the first place you have chosen. You will meet a wise woman. It is someone you admire but have never met—a biblical person, a member of the generation directly ahead of you, a character from a book or show, a favorite writer. Who is your wise woman? Tell her of your difficulty and see if she has any thoughts to share with you about it.

Go to the second place and meet a wise and understanding woman you know or have known. You may choose a family member, friend, counselor, or neighbor. She is waiting for you—both to listen to you and to offer her accepting love. Tell her of your difficulty. Listen to her response and experience her loving care for you.

At the third place find your woman-friend-God (in whatever form She takes) waiting for you. Bring your difficulty to Her. Receive Her love and whatever She offers you.

Psalm Parallel (Psalm 22)

My God, my Mother, have you, too, abandoned me?
I can barely pray.
For all my crying, I can't find words.
I have been calling to you day after day.
You haven't answered me.
I wrestle during the night and cannot sleep,
But you bring me no relief.
Our mothers trusted in you.
They put their trust in you and were saved.

Worries about the present and the future
    form a net around me.
My fear ties up the corners
    and traps my trust in you.
Others call me foolish
And say that prayer is nothing,
    nothing at all:
"If She is your good,
Let Her rescue you,
If She loves you."

You have been my guide since I was small
    my security since my mother held me in her arms.
To you I was called from birth;
You are my God since my mother's womb
Be close to me in time of trouble.
Be near, for no one else can help me.

In my circle of friends I will praise you.
I will praise your name to everyone,
"You who are in awe of God, praise Her;
You will find Her faithful and ever loving,
She will not turn Her face from you
When you, too, cry out to Her."

PERSONAL RITUAL

Find a stone a little larger than your hand.
Name the ways—the good ways—you are like this stone.
Smear mud on it.
With your finger, trace the name or make a symbol in the mud for your own personal mud—some fault, sin, compulsion, or addiction.

Dip your stone in a bowl of water or place it under running water. Let this action be a sign of the cleansing of your spirit by the One who loves you.

Keep your stone in a prominent place and let it remind you that you are cleansed in and by Her love. Allow it to remind you that your sin is forgiven.

COMMON RITUAL

This prayer/ritual should symbolize these three truths:
The basic goodness of each person present.
Recognition that sinfulness, faults, and omissions have marred individual potential for good.
The cleansing forgiveness received in the love of God who is Sister, Friend, and Mother.

Materials Needed

One object for each participant to symbolize the goodness of each person—an apple, a stone, a simulated pearl (available in fabric or craft shops), a large leaf. If you have fourteen people, for example, you could use fourteen apples or a mixture of items adding up to fourteen.

An ordinary, well-used kitchen utensil such as a large pan, a Dutch oven, or a mixing bowl filled with mud.

A large, lovely bowl (preferably opaque) filled with clean water. (In a clear bowl, the muddy water will be visible.)

A small round table.

Hand towel(s).

A tape or record of soft, instrumental music, as well as other musical selections as indicated.

Paper plates or waxed paper.

Preparation

Give each person a symbol of his or her goodness. Suggest that each participant find a private place to pray and to think about how this object reflects him or her. (For example, an apple is nourishing, solid, available year round, beautiful; a stone has history, sparkle, color, strength, dependability; a pearl is precious, luminous, and especially lovely when part of a group on a necklace.) Give the group fifteen to thirty minutes for reflection.

As people return, play soft instrumental music to preserve the quiet reflective atmosphere. Position one chair for each person in a circle around a small table. Place the container of mud nearby, but keep the mud concealed until needed.

Ritual

When everyone is seated, offer the following thoughts:

> Our God has made all Her daughters and sons beautiful. Each of us is one of a kind in the gifts and goodness given to us. We praise Her by recognizing our gifts and acknowledging the gifts of others.
>
> Each of us has looked at ourselves and looked at the *(object)* to see what we had in common with it. Would some of you please share with the rest of us some of the ways you found yourself like the *(object)*?

(If sixty seconds yields no sharing, the leader can begin with the result of his or her meditation, saying "I am like this *(object)* because..." or "This *(object)* reminds me of myself because...")

When sharing is completed, the leader puts the kitchen container of mud on the table in the center of the circle. Uncover the mud and let each person see it. Speak of the muddiness of the world into which each is born, the imperfection of our families of origin, the dirt kicked up by the tensions and conflicts of daily living, the smears of our own poor choices that stain and mar and blur the goodness in each of us as represented by the *(object)*. To acknowledge this truth, ask each person to bring his or her *(object)* forward individually. Take each, dip it in the mud, and give it back (on a paper plate or waxed paper or other protective holder).

As each person comes forward, address him or her with the following or similar words:

> You were born of the earth into a world of light
> and darkness. You share in its muddiness as well as
> its beauty. Ask God to show you your particular clots
> of mud that you may be cleansed of them, that your
> beauty may shine more fully.

After all have returned to their chairs, ask them to leave the circle, find a private place, and spend a designated time (fifteen to forty minutes) considering what comprises their own personal mud. Assure them that they will not be asked to share with the group anything they wish to keep to themselves.

Before the group members return, replace the container of mud with the bowl of clean water and some towels. Nearby, place a container for the plates or papers on which the muddy objects have been carried. Again play gentle, meditative music as people return. When all are seated, sing "Be Near Me, O God" from *Cry of Ramah* by Colleen Fulmer (see Appendix B). Ask a few warm-up questions such as: Did you find this time difficult or easy? Why do you think it was so? What are your feelings at this time? (This warm-up need not last long. No one should be telling the group what he or she discovered during this time—only the general experience of meditating on sinfulness.)

Speak of the great love our Mother or Friend or Sister-God has for each of us. Read some of the following quotations (one person could read these or the quotations could be prepared by two or three persons who read them from their places in the circle—with thirty to sixty seconds of silence between):

I will sprinkle clean water upon you to
cleanse you from all your impurities (Eze 36:25).

I will give you a new heart and place a
new spirit within you, taking from your bodies
your stony hearts and giving you natural hearts
(Eze 36:26).

Fear not, for I have redeemed you;
    I have called you by name: you are
        mine (Is 43:1).

I will give you treasures out of the darkness,
and riches that have been hidden away,
That you may know that I am the LORD,
    the God of Israel, who calls you by
        your name (paraphrase of Is 45:1,3).

Your sins are forgiven. . . . Which is easier,
to say . . . "Your sins are forgiven," or to say,
"Rise, pick up your mat and walk"? (Mk 2:5,9).

Jesus said, "Neither do I condemn you. Go,
from now on do not sin any more" (Jn 8:11).

[Jesus] said to her, "Daughter, your faith
has saved you; go in peace" (Lk 8:48).

Though your sins be like scarlet,
    they may become white as snow;
Though they be crimson red,
    they may become white as wool (Is 1:18).

Invite members to bring their symbols to the
center—individually. Either before or as they do so,
ask them to offer some variation on the following
prayer:

I bring myself and the mud of (*They can
name the mud; for example, "my impatience," "my*

struggle against self-doubt," "my inclination to think
only of my own feelings and not of others." Or they
can say "the mud of my faults" or "the mud of my
sins.") and ask God's healing. I trust in Her love
and Her cleansing.

The leader then takes the muddy symbol, dips it into the
water, dries it, and returns it to the participant.
Option 1:   If the group has demonstrated a high level of trust, the
individual coming forward could ask for someone to pray with
him or her for cleansing. Another member of the group (instead
of the leader) could come forward as an act of friendship to pray
and dip the symbol in the water.
Option 2:   Another leader could read a scripture quotation (and/
or give a copy of it) to the person who has just received the
cleansed symbol.

When all are seated, invite the group members to offer brief
spontaneous prayers—of thanksgiving, of petition for one another,
of offering of self, and so on.

Close with "Mother Earth" or "Shaddai" from *WomanSong*
by Miriam Therese Winter, or "El Shaddai" from *Cry of Ramah* by
Colleen Fulmer (see Appendix B).

Mirroring Her

Opening Prayer

O God, we see your reflection everywhere—in the emerging crocuses in spring, in the caverns carved out for thousands of years under the earth, in the glowing white hair of a grandmother, in the pebbled face of a mosaic, in the sand castle of a child. You are everywhere. Sometimes we fail to recognize your presence. Sometimes we obscure it.

Help us to find you most gloriously in our sisters and brothers as they make you present in their persons and personalities. Show us your face—in one another.

GUIDED IMAGERY MEDITATION

We will come to a better understanding of the feminine side of God by thinking of women whose godly qualities have contributed to our well-being, our enjoyment, our inspiration, and our healing as persons and as a society.

You will be familiar with the names of some of the women, yet many will be unknown to you since our patriarchal society does not usually put the gifts of women into the context of history.

Imagine a great stretch of land, a great field from which you can see to the horizon in every direction around you. This setting provides the grounds for you to discover more about God. You will be able to find Her feminine qualities by reflecting on women She has created. As each woman is named, and as you see her name, place her on this great field in the presence of God, who created her in Her own image and likeness. To do this, you do not have to image the woman's physical appearance. Rather, hold a general sense of the person in her gifts and accomplishments.

Nearly all of the women we will place here are real people. A few, however, are mythical women who reflect the feminine qualities collected from the conscious and subconscious of many centuries. One such figure is the great Goddess revered by the people of Europe and the people of the Near and Far East for at least nine thousand years before the Christian Era and for almost three centuries into it. Some of her titles were Creator of the Heavens and the Earth, Lady of the Universe, and Mother Above All Gods. Her name, in various languages, is Eurynome, Tiamat, Nammu, Ishtar, Isis, Astarte, Ashtoreth or Ianna. She was the goddess of birth and rebirth, worshiped as the source of life, of nourishment, of protection, of warmth. She reigned supreme over all other gods. Place this Goddess image on the field.

In earlier cultures, including the Jewish, wisdom was perceived as feminine. As Sophia, she represented the transformation of female power into a pure spiritual dimension. In the Bible only the names of God and Jesus appear more frequently than that of Sophia. Place her on the field.

In our Judeo-Christian tradition we look to women both real and fictional to reflect to us other aspects of God:

Miriam, a leader of her people, a support in faith and in prayer for her brother Moses.

Ruth and Naomi, examples of loving faithfulness among women.

Deborah, a prophet and judge.

Esther, a queen willing to lay down her life for the salvation of her people.

Sarah, mother of the nation called Israel.

Mary, biological and nurturing mother of Jesus and spiritual mother of His followers.

What other biblical woman captures your imagination? Place her on the field with the others. What qualities of God does she suggest?

Think of women who share in God's creativity. Let us recognize women who expand our sensitivity as they offer us their creative visions in the arts: Matilda of Flanders, eleventh-century creator of the Bayeaux Tapestry; Gisela of Kerzenbroech, illuminator of manuscripts, and Joanna, weaver, both of thirteenth-century Germany; Elizabeth Lucar, sixteenth-century English calligrapher; Artemisia Gentileschi and all of the women painters and artists of Renaissance Italy who were never entered into the art history recorded by male art historians; nineteenth- and twentieth-century artists Mary Cassatt, Elizabeth Nourse, Georgia O'Keefe, Louise Nevelson, Louise Bourgeois, Judy Chicago, Maya Ying Lin.

Think of an artistic woman whom you know; for instance, one who arranges flowers well, or someone who is an excellent decorator, or an art teacher or potter. Place her, too, on this field. How does she reflect God to you?

God reveals the secrets of Her universe slowly
through those who discover them. Among great
women scientists we recall Caroline Herschel, discoverer of a comet; Maria Cunitz, seventeenth-century
German astronomer; Sophie Germain, eighteenth-
century French mathematician; Mother Hutton,
nineteenth-century English biologist and pharma-
cist who discovered how to use digitalis medically;
Josephine Kublick, a paleontologist of nineteenth-
century Czechoslovakia; Madame Curie, discoverer
of radium; her daughter Irene Joliot-Curie, discoverer
of the neutron; Emmy Noether, twentieth-century
mathematician.

Think of a woman whom you know—or one of
whom you have heard—who has studied a science,
does research, or teaches mathematics. As you place
her with the others on the field, meditate on how she
reflects something of God to you.

Can you see a God who desires to give Her
healing to us through the many women of many
centuries—physicians, nurses, health care profession-
als? Remember that these persons frequently faced
persecution, insult, and oppression as they tried to
gain and use a knowledge of medicine to effect God's
healing in others. Think about Agnodice, a gynecol-
ogist of the sixth century before the Christian era;
Aspasia of Athens, a surgeon in Greece four hundred
years before the Christian Era; Berthildis, Ethelberga,
and Ethelreda of seventh-century Europe, who were
among the abbesses sought for their knowledge of the
healing arts; Adelberger, eighth-century Italian physician; Francesca of Salerno, fourteenth-century Italian
surgeon; and the thousands of women throughout
the thirteenth to the seventeenth centuries who used
the healing powers of the herbs and minerals of
nature and who were hanged or burned at the stake
as witches because it was unacceptable for women to
have the power of knowledge.

Reflect upon Angelizue du Coudray, obstetrician of eighteenth-century France; Clara Barton, founder of the American Red Cross; Emily and Elizabeth Blackwell, who pioneered medical training for women in the nineteenth-century United States; Rebecca Lee, the first black woman physician; Susan Flesche Piccottee, Native American physician; and Florence Nightingale, nursing and medical pioneer.

Think for a few moments of a woman you know who uses her knowledge of medicine or her nursing or health care skills to bring the healing power of God to greater fullness.

Consider some women whose musical abilities reflect a God who creates just for pleasure and expression. Composer Hildegarde of Bingen of twelfth-century Germany, who was also a medical woman, scientist, writer, abbess, and saint; Marguerite Louise Couperin, musician and singer of seventeenth-century France; Faustine Bordini, opera singer of eighteenth-century Italy; Jenny Lind, nineteenth-century singer; Clara Schumann, composer and great pianist of nineteenth-century Germany; Mary Lou Williams, jazz pianist, arranger, and composer; and familiar twentieth-century singers Marian Anderson, Barbra Streisand, Beverly Sills, Pearl Bailey, composer Ethel Smyth, and dancers and choreographers Martha Graham and Suzanne Farrell.

Think of a woman you know who is gifted in playing an instrument or in composing music or in singing or dancing well. What does she reveal of God?

Women who exerted great influence over individuals and societies in religion did so despite prejudice and pressure leveled against them by the men—and often the women—of their times. Bridget, sixth-century Irish feminist, helped spread Christianity throughout Ireland and established education centers for women; Julian of Norwich, fourteenth-century English mystic and writer; Catherine of Siena,

reformer and political leader; Clare of Assisi, religious
reformer, founder, ascetic; Teresa of Avila, reformer,
founder, religious leader, doctor of the church; Anne
Hutchinson, preacher with the seventeenth-century
Puritan community; Mother Ann Lee, founder of
American Shaker communities; Mary Baker Eddy,
founder of Christian Science; Evelyn Underhill, An-
glican spiritual writer and guide; Elizabeth Seton,
Catherine McAuley, Katharine Drexel, women whose
charity and vision led to the founding of large communities of women who dedicated their lives to
works of mercy; scripture scholars Pheme Perkins
and Elizabeth Schüssler Fiorenza; Mother Teresa of
Calcutta, Nobel Prize winner for spreading the message of love by her actions and words; Rosemary
Ruether, Sandra Schneiders, and all those who call
and lead women to use the fullness of their gifts in
the church.

Consider a woman you know whom you consider a religious leader or spiritual guide. What
qualities of God does she radiate? Place her with all
the other Spirit-filled women on the field.

Among great women rulers who have guided
their countries through stormy political waters recall
Elizabeth I and Queen Victoria of England, Margaret
of Scotland, Isabella of Spain, Catherine the Great of
Russia, Golda Meir of Israel.

Although many women's books have endured
the test of time to become literary classics, the
women writers sometimes had to assume masculine pen names to get their work published. A
few of the writers are Hrosvitha, tenth-century
playwright, Emily Dickinson, the Bronte sisters,
Mary Ann Evans, Elizabeth Barrett Browning, Jane
Austen, Sigrid Undset, Flannery O'Connor, Al-
ice Walker, Adrienne Rich, Nikki Giovanni, and
Annie Dillard. Include contemporary humorists

who help us laugh at ourselves—columnist Erma Bombeck and cartoonist Cathy Guisewite, creator of *Cathy.*

Name a woman you know who writes well. How does she speak of the reality of God through her person in the use of her gifts? Place her on the field with all the other wonderful women writers.

Name a few great women who were, or are, researchers, pioneers, or innovators in their fields: Karen Horney, psychiatrist; Jane Goodall, anthropologist; Maria Montessori, educator; Margaret Mead, anthropologist and social psychologist; Amelia Earhart, pioneer aviator; and Sally Ride, astronaut.

Against great odds women have built, owned, and managed their own businesses: Lydia of the New Testament, who bought and sold cloth expensively dyed in purple; Damelis, ninth-century Byzantine businesswoman; Kenau Hasselaer, sixteenth-century shipwright of Holland; Barbara Uttman, founder of the lace industry in sixteenth-century Germany; Margaret Philipse, shipowner in seventeenth-century United States; Mary Goddart, printer and publisher in the United States in the eighteenth century; Victoria Woodhull, nineteenth-century United States stockbroker; Esther Ocullo, founder of the first food factory in Ghana; Mary Kay Asche, founder of Mary Kay Cosmetics; Liz Claiborne, the first woman whose company made the Fortune 500 list; and all women today who have begun their own businesses or who manage business or financial institutions.

Think of a woman you know who is making a contribution to the business world. As you place her on the field with the rest, consider what qualities of God she reflects.

Do you have room for some athletes on your field? Place there Cynisca, Spartan athlete from the third century before the Christian era; Juliana Berners, fifteenth-century expert in hunting, hawking, and fishing; Sophia Heath, who opened the Olympics to women in 1912; Elin Kallio, who founded the first athletic association in Northern Europe.

In recognition of all the marvelous women athletes of the twentieth century, place on the field Babe Didrikson Zaharias, Althea Gibson, and Joan Benoit, Sonja Henie and Katarina Witt, Olga Korbut, Nadia Comaneci, and Mary Lou Retton, Chris Evert and Martina Navratilova, Nancy Lopez, Annemarie Proell Moser.

If you have another favorite athlete, add her to the group. And name an athletic woman you know. Think about the gifts that reflect God as you place her on the field.

Any woman who chooses to fight the injustices of the political and social systems will experience the leaders of these systems trying to crush her. Consider the courage and stamina, as well as the inner power of conviction, shown by women such as Sojourner Truth, abolitionist and feminist; Susan B. Anthony, Elizabeth Cady Stanton, Margaret Brent, and Mary Otis Warren, all nineteenth-century activists who challenged injustices and finally claimed for United States women their right to vote; Harriet Beecher Stowe, writer, abolitionist, suffragist; Harriet Tubman, Jane Addams, Eleanor Roosevelt, social reformers; Rachel Carson, environmentalist; Simone de Beauvoir, feminist writer; Corazon Aquino and all women struggling to bring about justice in their homelands; Dorothy Day, social and political activist; Coretta Scott King, leader for black equality in the United States; Maura Clarke, Jean Donovan, Dorothy Kazel, and Ita Ford, slain for working to liberate the oppressed in El Salvador; Theresa Kane, who publicly challenged her church's hierarchy for excluding women from full ministry; Maggie Kuhn, who founded the Gray Panthers to fight injustices toward aging persons.

Think of a woman you know who is fighting
oppression of some kind and acting to promote
justice. Place her, too, on the field and decide what
qualities of God you see in her.

Recall a woman in your family who has had a
positive influence on you. What facet of God do you
see in her? Place her on the field. Consider a woman
in your friendship circle whom you respect or admire
or love. Place her on the field as you consider what
aspects of God she radiates.

Of the traits that you consider to be feminine,
which one do you like or appreciate or admire the
most? In some way, image or sense God with that
trait.

Look at the field around you—this great plain
filled with the women of whom we have spoken.
Add all of their gifted contemporaries we have not
mentioned. Add gifted women from Africa, Central,
and South America and other places around the
world—women whose memories are eclipsed by
both sexism and nationalism.

See these women with all of the gifted women
who are *your* contemporaries, people who are using
and expanding their talents and skills for the good of
their families, churches, schools, community, nation,
and world. Look around this field now and see
women without number and without end on all
sides. See them suffused in light, an embrace of light
that both surrounds the women and arises from them.
Bring the feminine within you to this gathering, enter
the field, and stand with the others suffused in the
light. This light is a part of all and yet more than all.
Each of you, all of you, are part of Her.

Hear a voice from within the light saying to
you and to all the women who stand with you: "You
are my beloved. I am so pleased with you." Live
in Her light with the others. Live in the embracing,
nurturing, powerful feminine side of God.[1]

Reflection/Discussion Starters

What is your reaction to the fact that God was worshiped as female for thousands of years before the Judeo-Christian tradition emerged?

Who was the additional biblical woman you chose to place on the field?

Who was the person you added in art? Mathematics or science? Music? Health care? Social justice? Spiritual leadership? Politics? Writing? Athletics? Research? Business?

Many or most of the women were probably unknown to you. What feelings did this evoke in you?

Why have so many outstanding women been left out of history books?

What women other than those mentioned would you like to add?

What woman in your family did you add to the list? What woman in your circle of friends?

Describe the field as you pictured it at the end of your meditation.

Did this meditation hold any surprises for you—intellectual or emotional or spiritual? If so, what are they?

FOR PERSONAL PRAYER

Recognizing Her

Make a list of five to ten women you know. Next to each name, write a special quality or gift or skill the woman possesses. Hold your list reverently and picture each person. As you do so, recognize her as an expression of God. Thank God for this glimpse of Her.

Write down some of your own special qualities or gifts or skills. Recognize yourself as an expression of Her. Then let yourself rest in knowing that not only do your qualities reflect God, but your very person, your very self, is a reflection of Her. You flow from Her being.

Experiencing Her

Choose a "non-person" image of God such as light or warmth or a cloud.

Let yourself feel embraced by this image. Let it penetrate you from the outside and radiate from you on the inside. Rest in Her without words.

Psalm Parallel (Psalm 8)

O God, our nurturing Mother,
Your very name sounds wonderful.
You show your strength and your glory
    in the heavens
    and all over the land.
Children and babies
    cry out in response to you.
And unbelievers are taken aback,
    unable to explain what they see.
When I look at the sky painted by your hands,
    the moon and the stars you sculpted within it,
I wonder what I am—that you should even think of me—
    or my children that you should care for them.

You have made me far less than an angel,
Yet called me to share in your work.
You have given me power
    to bring forth life.
You have given me love
    to nurture its growth.

All the earth is creative
    and shares in your life-giving power.

Women and men, sparrows and camels,
  dolphins and katydids, hawks and turtles—
You call all of us to create,
  to nourish life,
  to rejoice in being.
O nurturing God,
Thank you!
Your very name sounds wonderful.

PERSONAL RITUAL

Draw a circle on a piece of paper.

Ask Her to show you what you most contribute to those around you, what qualities of Her you radiate.

Within the circle, use colored pens or chalk or crayons to draw that gift or a symbol of the gift.

Keep the circle before you for a week. Be aware each day that this gift is both Hers and yours.

COMMON RITUAL
(For a Group of Women)

This works best when participants know each other fairly well. It is still affirming, however, if people have participated in groups together during the day.

Preparation

If the group numbers more than ten, divide into smaller groups. Sit in circles or around tables.

Provide each participant with a pencil and a piece of paper with circles drawn on it. The number of circles should correspond to the number of people in the group.

Option: Instead of circles, use globes, pennants, long streamers, or balloons.

Ritual

A leader explains that each person present has talents and skills she shares with others. Often a woman is unaware of them herself. Women so often undervalue their own gifts. This time of prayer is intended to illuminate one another's gifts and the contributions the participants make to the lives of others.

Ask each participant to write the name of each person in the group in the center of a circle—one name per circle. Then direct the participants to find a quiet, individual place to think and pray about the other members of the group. During the next twenty minutes, each participant should envision one person after another and recall some of her gifts, qualities, or skills—at least two for each person. If anyone finishes early, use the time to envision each person again and say a prayer for each one.

While the participants are doing this, a leader hangs a large circle for each person in the group room on the walls (or on a board or some s of a participant is in each circle. Play reflect es an atmosphere of prayer as people come all groups.

When all have return pencils or pens and ask the participants to ach person and to write in that circle the w ritten on their smaller circles. Alternately, t e taped to the larger circle.

Play music with some j pants move around the room.

Lower the volume of the shift to more meditative music to signal a return to the circles.

A leader removes the large circles from the wall and gives each person the one with her name on it. Request silence during this time of reading.

A leader then tells the group that reading one's gifts is one kind of experience. Listening to one's gifts is another.

Ask each group to focus on one member while the other members, one by one, name her qualities, gifts, or skills. These qualities may be the ones the speaker previously listed, or she may add others. For instance, "Dorothy, I think you listen better than anyone I know." "Sharon, you are always open to new ideas." "Carol, I love the way you treat each of your children—and everyone else—with so much respect."

Third-person statements ("I think Joyce adds joy to our group with her spirit of hopefulness") are not appropriate. The speaker should look directly at Joyce and say, "Joyce, I think you add...." Disclaimers by the person being addressed are also inappropriate. A simple thank you is an adequate response.

When all of this is completed, a leader may ask if anyone wishes to express her feelings. Again, don't allow any disclaimers. Some may express surprise or joy or speak of the difficulty of giving or receiving compliments.

A leader closes by reminding everyone that "where Love is, there is God" and that Her presence is manifest among us in the love and respect shown to one another.

Invite participants to give some sign of peace to one another and then close with "Magnificat" or "Women" or "You Are The Song" from *WomanSong* by Miriam Therese Winter, "Circling Free" from *Circling Free* by Marsie Silvestro, or "Woman in the Night" from *Faith Looking Forward* by Brian Wren (see Appendix B).

---

[1] For this meditation, I received inspiration—and information—from that wonderful art exhibit and book called *The Dinner Party*. I am grateful to Judy Chicago and her group of researchers, artists, and artisans.

Imaging Her

Opening Prayer

God, you are the source of all that is feminine
and all that is masculine. You are the source of all
that we know and understand. Yet you are beyond
all our knowing and understanding.

When we think about you, we are confronted
with the limits of our minds. When we prepare
to speak about you, we realize the poverty of our
language. When we try to imagine you, the best we
can do is to conjure up symbols, which only hint of
your Being.

We try to reach you in prayer. We ask you to
come to us, to teach us about yourself, and to show
us where and how to find you.

Teach us about the feminine in you and in
ourselves. Show us how all that is feminine is
rooted in you—and how your feminine qualities are
enfleshed in us. Help us as we open ourselves to you
in symbols, in images, and words. Let your Spirit use
these poor treasures of ours to deepen our knowledge
of you.

GUIDED IMAGERY MEDITATION

A symbol speaks to us of a truth or an experience for which we cannot find appropriate words—or it calls to consciousness a truth we half-perceive or one we know in a subconscious part of ourselves. For instance, a stone picked up on a lakeshore may evoke images of the water or the feelings of freedom felt on vacation.

Symbols can connect us to deep and universal truths. Looking at a cross calls up our awareness of suffering and salvation. Water lapping on the sand may be a sign of cleansing for some, or death for others, or loneliness, or peace. A butterfly or lily often evokes the joy of new beginnings, of new life.

To prepare yourself for this reflective exercise, responding to a collage of feminine symbols, find a comfortable, quiet place where you can relax. As you do so, however, remember to do whatever is necessary to also maintain your alertness. Sitting in a straight-backed chair and keeping your feet on the floor helps to achieve this. Be sure you are able to breathe freely.

Slowly take a breath. Breathe again and, without forcing it, let your breathing become a little deeper. Breathe slowly and deeply for one or two minutes.

In order to deepen relaxation, visualize the following symbols. Let each appear at a distance in a mist. Let it appear very small and see it drift gradually toward you, becoming larger. Then watch it fade away.

First, picture a silver ring...

then a bowl...

a cup...

an egg...

a pot of soil . . .

a seashell . . .

a woven basket.

Remember also that words are symbols. They are letters on paper or sounds from our lips that call up images and ideas in the minds of listeners.

Remember too that—like the word *father*—the word *mother*, when spoken of God, is a metaphor, a symbol we use to express our belief that our existence flows from God and that God is like a wonderful parent who gives us unconditional love.

One of the Hebrew names for God—*El Shaddai*—appears forty-eight times in the Hebrew Scriptures. It may be translated as "The Breasted One" or "The God with Breasts." The name may be a leftover from an earlier time when God was thought of as feminine or the name may reflect an earlier belief that God dwelled on the mountain or in the mountains. *El Shaddai* is often invoked in connection with fertility and with the feminine and nurturing aspects of God. If the image of *El Shaddai*, the God with Breasts, appeals to you, spend some time with Her on the mountain.

Look at other feminine images to see if they call up from your depths any sense of the feminine Creator. In the following, use only the symbol or symbols that appeal to you.

Look at an earthenware cup. It may recall the receptivity of our God, Her willingness to be part of our earthbound lives, Her desire to nourish us from Her fullness.

In like manner, how is a crystal bowl also a symbol of Her, of our God?

Ponder the image of a woman spinning and then weaving. Watch her at the wheel and then at the loom. Does she suggest any ways of God?

Speak to this Spinner-Weaver-God if you experience Her as a part of your life.

The symbols of mother are scattered throughout the Bible. Listen to two of them. This first one is from the Book of Numbers:

Moses asked the LORD..."Was it I who conceived all this people? or was it I who gave them birth, that you tell me to carry them at my bosom?" (Num 11:11, 12).

Let your mother God carry *you* for a while.

The second is from Isaiah:

As a mother comforts her son,
so will I comfort you (Is 66:13).

Do you need any comforting right now? If so, let God comfort you as Her son or daughter.

The Book of Hosea (13:8) has quite a different image of our Mother-God: God is like a mother bear robbed of her cubs.

I will attack [the idolaters]...
and tear their hearts from their
breasts (Hos 13:8)

says the word of the Lord. Does your God have any qualities like this angry mother bear?

Jesus gives us an image of Himself as a bird. He desires, He says, to gather Jerusalem as a mother bird collects her young under her wings. What qualities of Jesus, and therefore of God, do you find here?

How is the feminine image of an "enclosed garden" like our God?

Consider the egg as a feminine symbol. Does it speak to any aspect of God to you?

Picture a well. In what ways is a well a feminine symbol? In what ways might it speak of God?

Dwell on the dove, often a symbol of God's Spirit. What are the feminine qualities we associate with the dove?

A cave, like a womb, signifies the feminine. Is our God like a cave, or a cave like our God?

Choose the symbol or image that most speaks to you, most appeals to you: an earthen cup, crystal bowl, spinner and weaver, enclosed garden, egg, well, dove, cave, or another image of your own.

Hold that image before you. Let the femininity within you become one with that image. Spend time with it, and let it speak to you of yourself and of God. Then, when you are ready, let the union of yourself and the image become one with God within you and let yourself rest in union with Her.

C   ⸱⸱⸱ʳ⸱⸱⸱g to the group some of the symbols
r   Add some more of your own. Ask
t   ʳmbols in a quiet, relaxed, and cen-
t   ꓳ ꓝꓯⅠꓔ   ʄicient reflection, ask them to share
a   ꞏ to them.
                                this meditation with "Bring Many
]   *nes*, or "God of Many Names" from
                                ꞏian Wren (see Appendix B).

Reflection/Discussion Starters

What is a symbol? What do symbols do for us? How are words, as well as objects, symbols?

Does imaging God as mother change your sense of relationship to God? If so, how?

Do you find any qualities in God that are like an angry mother bear? If so, what are they?

How is each of these symbols both feminine and God-like?

A crystal bowl

A spinner and weaver

An enclosed garden

An egg

A well

A dove

A cave

To which symbol or image are you most attracted? Why?

How are the words *father* or *mother* symbolic when they are used in calling upon God?

Scripture: Numbers 11:11–12 (like a mother); Psalm 131:2 (like a child); Hosea 13:8 (like a bear); and Luke 13:34 (like a bird).

FOR PERSONAL PRAYER

Connecting With Your Symbol

Find a symbol that you would describe as feminine, perhaps a round object or shape to suggest a womb or breasts; an open vessel—like a bowl or a vase—that offers hospitality, that exists to be filled; or an egg or egg-shaped object that symbolizes fertility, the power to conceive life.

Hold the symbol in your hand. Look at its shape and texture and design. Feel its shape and texture. What differences do you see when you look at it from a distance or closely? Let yourself feel connected with this symbol.

Consider the feminine qualities your symbol suggests. How do these qualities exist in God? How do you express them? Feel your connection with God if you share the same qualities, if you enflesh them for Her in some way.

Speak to Her about the way you feel about your feminine qualities.

In God, in Jesus, in You

Take your bible to a quiet place and relax for a few minutes by paying attention to anything round, egg-shaped, or receptive (vase, flowerpot) around you. Look at the objects, touch them, and notice their details. Then open your bible to Luke 13:34 to read how Jesus uses the symbol of a mother hen to express how He feels. Think about the feminine qualities of Jesus in this passage.

What feminine qualities do you share in common with Jesus? How do both of you reflect Her? Speak with God or J

Closing Prayer

Psalm Parallel (Psalm 62)

Only in God does my spirit rest.
In Her I find my salvation.
She alone is my home and my fireplace,
My garden enclosed where I feel safe,
The breasts at which I will be nourished.
A woman or a man is only a breath;
Power and riches fly like the dust.
Trust not in promises of power.
Though wealth approach, do not claim it with your heart.
Two things only: the power of God to love,
The riches of God to be shared in kindness.

PERSONAL RITUAL

Consider the questions listed in the preparation section of the Common Ritual below. Find a symbol for a feminine quality in yourself. Think about how this exists in some way in God also. Enshrine your symbol in a place where you will notice it. Let it call you to reflect on your oneness with God.

COMMON RITUAL

Preparation

Each member of the group receives the following four questions:

What qualities do I consider feminine?
How do I see these qualities in God?

What are my strongest feminine qualities (one or two)?
How do I feel about these qualities in myself?

Ask each person to answer the questions privately and then
to find a symbol for one of the strongest feminine qualities. (Symbols may be found in nature, in the room, in purses and pockets,
in pictures from books and magazines brought for this purpose.)
While everyone is doing this, prepare a circle of chairs and place a
round, plain sheet of paper or cloth on the floor. The sheet should
be large enough to hold not only the symbols of the group but to
show them to good advantage.

On each chair place a copy of the affirmation (see Ritual below). While this affirmation is simple, it can be reassuring to have
the text at hand.

Ritual

When all have returned and seated themselves, invite the
group to sing "Women" from *WomanSong* by Miriam Therese Winter (see Appendix B).

One person invites everyone to join hands and then offers
the following or a similar introduction:

> As we join in identifying our feminine qualities,
> we celebrate the presence of our God among us.
> Let us continue to revere Her and celebrate Her in
> each other.

Invite (but do not pressure) members of the group to share
their symbols, their strongest feminine qualities, and the way they
feel about these qualities in themselves. After doing so, each participant then places the symbol on the sheet of paper in the center.
As each person returns, all hold hands and say:

We reverence the quality of *(quality)* in you, *(name)*."

When all who wish to share have done so, the leader invites
the "silent" participants to place their symbols in the center. Then,
a member of the group offers the following conclusion or a similar
one:

We rejoice in all the feminine qualities of our sisters and brothers here and throughout the world. We thank our God for the gift of them and the way they place us in union with Her. May our love for all that is feminine provide signs of hope and new life for all.

Sing "Blessing Song," "Breath of God," or "Magnificat" from *WomanSong*. If the group is all women, these songs would also be suitable: "A New Day Dawns" from *WomanSong*, "A Blessing Song" from *Circling Free* by Marsie Silvestro, "A Woman in a World of Men" from *Bring Many Names* and "Who Is She?" from *Praising a Mystery*, both by Brian Wren (see Appendix B).

Kneading, Baking, and Breaking Prayer

Opening Prayer

My God, Jesus said you are like a bakerwoman who puts yeast into the flour. Give me the yeast of your Spirit to enliven me. Prepare me to be your bread. Knead me and forgive my resistance.

You are my Mother, my Sister, my Friend. Yet I want to be even closer to you. Let me be one with you as the yeast of your Spirit transforms all that I am. Worked by your hands, my life will become bread, your bread, to be broken and shared with others. As I live within you and you within me, we will nourish others with your presence, your comfort, your strength, your love.

GUIDED IMAGERY MEDITATION

The kingdom of heaven is like yeast that a woman took and mixed with three measures of

wheat flour until the whole batch was leavened
(Mt 13:33).

The yeast is the power of the Spirit of God, which
can make us, the flour, rise to heights otherwise
beyond our ability. And the bakerwoman is God,
who puts this leaven in each of us and among us so
that we may become bread for one another.

As you begin this meditation, find a comfortable,
relaxed, yet alert position. Be aware of your body at
each of its contact points with the furniture or floor.
Put a little pressure on each of those points and let
go, feeling the release of tension. Do it again. Press
your whole body against the floor or furniture—and
release. Breathe deeply and slowly.

As a way of relaxing further in preparation
for our prayer, picture different kinds of bread:
commercial white bread, homemade whole wheat,
a long loaf of rye, raisin bread, cinnamon bread, a
crusty loaf of French bread.

Imagine rows of loaves in a bakery oven. Smell
them baking. Look at them displayed on the bakery
shelves. Smell the aroma in the store. Watch as a loaf
is wrapped and sold.

Imagine a freshly baked loaf of bread recently
turned out of a baking pan. Touch its crust lightly.
Take a knife, cut a thick slice, and offer the piece to a
friend.

Now ponder the unleavened loaf of bread on the
table at the Last Supper. Watch Jesus take that loaf
and break off a piece and offer it to John, and break
another and give it to James, and another to Philip,
and so on.

Imagine a small group of Christians in someone's
home sitting around a table. A leader picks up the
bread and breaks it into pieces, offering one to every
person in the room. Watch as they all hold the bread
and eat it together as a symbol of the oneness of

their lives and their willingness to share themselves in memory of Jesus.

Now enter a kitchen of your choosing, perhaps your own or another with which you are familiar. Choose a place in which you would like to work. You are going to bake a loaf of bread. Use your imagination and follow these instructions.

First, open a drawer and take out an apron to protect your clothing from the flour. And, as you wash your hands, feel the frothy foam of the soap gliding over them.

Now you are going to get out your ingredients. Measure and place them within your reach: two packages of dry yeast, three tablespoons of shortening, three tablespoons of sugar, one tablespoon of salt. Place the flour at hand with a measuring cup alongside it. And finally, measure two cups of milk into a pan and heat it slowly to scalding. Let the milk cool.

Take out a large mixing bowl. Turn on the faucet and let your fingers feel the water running over them. Let it run until it is lukewarm, but not hot. Test the warmth of the water by flicking a few drops on your wrist. When it feels right, measure three-fourths cup into the mixing bowl.

Tear off the top of the yeast packages and let the yeast fall slowly into the water. Receive the smell of the dissolving yeast as it rises to greet you.

To this, add the sugar and feel its grittiness between the spoon and the bowl as you stir it in. Be aware of the smoothness of the blend as the grains dissolve. The sugar will feed the yeast, help it to grow and help to brown the crust of your bread. Add the salt now and know that the salt will keep the yeast from growing too much. Stir in the shortening and the cooled milk. As you mix all this, watch the changes of color and texture.

Slowly add several cups of flour and stir it in. Add more and feel the resistance as you increase the amount of flour. You must beat this mixture now until it feels smooth. It is hard work and you are aware of the muscles in your arms and wrists as you do this.

Your mixture is smooth now, so begin adding more flour very slowly. Add until you are able to pick up the dough and handle it.

Lightly dust flour on a surface in front of you. Feel its softness. Cover your hands with flour, too. Now lift the dough on to the surface. *Pause*, because this is a sacred moment. With people all over the world down through the centuries, you are about to knead your dough. Fold the dough toward you and push it away with the heels of your hands. Do it again. Fold it toward you, push it away. Again, with a rocking motion. Rotate the dough as you knead it. Pull and push. Fold and press. Pull and push. Fold and press. Do this for about ten minutes.

Feel the resistance as you first start to move and turn the dough. Feel it become more and more one with you, and more pliable as you continue to work with it. Your kneading is bringing this dough to life. It distributes the yeast, squeezes out the air, and gives the texture for baking. As you work the dough, continue to feel yourself moving in rhythm with it, becoming more one with it. Pull and push. Fold and press. Is your dough beginning to feel springy? You are almost finished. Your dough is ready if it has a satin-smooth surface that is blistered with tiny bubbles just underneath it.

Shape the dough into a ball. Lightly grease a large bowl and place the ball of dough in it. Cover it to avoid drafts and place it in a warm spot—the top of your stove, a radiator, or inside a just-warm oven that has been turned off.

It will take about an hour for your yeast dough to double its size. You may wish to rest or to do other tasks while you wait. Whatever you do, reflect for a while on what you have done to prepare your bread.

The time goes quickly. Go back to your dough, remove the cover, and look at the mound before you. Is it twice as high as it was? Admire this work of the yeast aided by your hands. But your instructions are to punch it down again, down to its earlier size. How do you feel about doing this? It must be done. So plunge your fist into the center of the dough and watch it collapse. This will release large air bubbles and your bread will have a firmer texture.

Put the dough back on your floured surface. Divide it in half and put each half into a greased loaf pan. Cover one of the pans with plastic wrap and place it in the refrigerator. You will bake this loaf sometime during the week.

Brush your remaining loaf with some melted butter or margarine. Cover it and let it rise again in a warm place—until it nearly doubles its size again. This will take about an hour, so sit down to think about the bread and the power of this yeast, the need to knead the yeast into the dough, the importance of punching down the dough after its first burst of growth, of expansion. Think of the need to do all these things so that the separate ingredients, which *you* put in, can become one nourishing loaf to enjoy and share.

As you rest, imagine yourself as this dough. First you are plain flour pounded from the grains of the earth. God, who prepares you, infuses you with the yeast of Her spirit so that you may rise and be transformed.

Let yourself be kneaded by your bakerwoman-God. Feel the caring touch of Her assurance of love, the correcting fingers of Her discipline to improve your texture. And let yourself, if you can, accept the punching down that comes from the circumstances of life so that your next rising may be firmer.

How do you feel about being kneaded? Do you feel Her touch as gentle? Or strong? Do you feel controlled? Or cared for? Can you feel the action of being pulled up from the bottom and folded over in the kneading? Does this happen in your life in any way? How do you respond to it? Do you let it happen? Offer resistance? Do you rise again?

Let Her push down some of your puffed-up parts so that you may rise again with more substance. Feel Her shape you and reshape you. And feel yourself filled with the power of the yeast, the power of the Spirit. This power is one with you, yet more than you.

With the writer of Ephesians, proclaim that the *power* now at work in you can do immeasurably more than you can ask or imagine (Eph 3:20).

Go back and look at your dough, doubled again. *Rejoice* in it. It is the right size now. It is ready for baking. Tuck it into a heated oven.

In about forty-five minutes you will tap the crust with your finger. A hollow sound means that your bread is properly baked. Your loaf will be ready then to be broken and shared with others, to give them nourishment and energy for life, to give them pleasure. And you, are you too ready to be broken and shared that you may nurture others with new life? Speak with the bakerwoman-God who guides you, nourishes you, and asks *you* to share in Her creative love by sustaining life in others.

Option for group leader: Before beginning the meditation, ask participants to share their bread-baking experiences.
Option for group leader: At the end of the meditation, bless and share a loaf of homemade bread. Sing or play a recording of "Companions on the Journey" from *Companions on the Journey* by Carey Landry (see Appendix B).

Reflection/Discussion Starters

What helped you to relax most in the opening exercise of seeing, smelling, and touching bread? What did you enjoy the most?

If you have baked bread, compare your experience with doing it in your imagination. If you haven't baked bread, were you able to enter into the details described? Into the action of kneading?

How did you feel about punching down the dough when it had doubled its size?

What experiences of being "punched down" have you had in life? In what ways are you changed because of them?

How does it feel to be "kneaded and shaped" by God? Did you have a sense of God as feminine in this action?

How are you called to *be* bread?

How is a Christian community called to *be* bread?

How is the bakerwoman an appropriate image for God?

Scripture: Matthew 13:33 (the kingdom of heaven is like yeast); Ephesians 3:20 (God's power at work in us).

FOR PERSONAL PRAYER

Joining in the Baking of Bread

If you are able to claim several hours of quiet for yourself, bake a loaf of bread. Do so unhurriedly, observant of each ingredient, aware of each step in the process. Be aware of all you touch and how it feels. Breathe in the smells. Hear the sounds.

During the times for the rising of the dough, consider some of the following:

♦ Your connection with others who are baking bread for themselves and their families all over the world. Imagine them as they use modern ovens, adobe ovens, open fires. Watch them making various kinds of bread—pita, tortilla, French loaves, pancakes, crepes, croissants, whole wheat buns. See them in the image of Her, baking this bread as an expression of Her nurturing.

♦ Your connection with all women and men breaking bread down through the ages—in neolithic times, classical civilizations, African tribes, medieval Europe, nineteenth-century India. Visualize Muslims at the time of Mohammed, Chinese peoples who sat at the feet of the Buddha, twelfth-century Hopewell Indians in the U.S. Midwest, the Mayans of Mexico, eighteenth-century Russians, and so on. All of humanity is bound by the making, the baking, the breaking, and the sharing of bread. See all of them in the image of God. Be aware of Her baking the bread with them.

♦ Your oneness with Her as She bakes the bread with you.

Her Power in You

Choose a quiet place and relax a few moments by looking at an object or something of nature around you. Notice the details, the color, the textures, the shape. Be aware of Her presence with you and in you.

Read Ephesians 3:14–21, changing the masculine pronouns for God to feminine ones. Reread the passage several times, letting your mind or your heart be attracted to any word or phrase. As this happens, let the particular word or phrase dwell in you. Speak to Her about the power that She offers you.

The Bread of Life

Follow the steps described above until you get to the reading. Read John 6 instead. Read it slowly several times, changing the masculine language for God to feminine, and the words for human beings from masculine ones to those which include both sexes; for example, change "all men" to "all people." If a phrase holds you, stay with it.

"Take and Eat"

Follow the steps described above until you get to the reading. Use Matthew 26:26 instead. Read the whole passage slowly several times. Then begin repeating Jesus' words over and over, either silently or within yourself. Try saying them in rhythm with your breathing.

Psalm Parallel (Psalm 127)

Unless a family is centered in God,
It labors in vain to build a home of love.
Unless She lives within the house,
In vain do they strive for peace.
It is vain to be working all the time
And not take time for rest.
She calls those who work for bread
To rest in one another—and in Her.
Children are a gift from Her.
The fruit of the womb is a blessing.
Like flowers fresh and blooming
Are the children of one's youth.
Happy is the woman whose arms are full.
She shall not be alone
When old age knocks on her door.

PERSONAL RITUAL

Hold a piece of bread in your hands. Eat it slowly, aware of your union with people all over the world who are eating some form of bread today. Think of them as your brothers and sisters in Her.

COMMON RITUAL

Either of the following rituals can stand alone. If a group is going to be together for a day, however, both rituals may be used, one early in the day and one at the end.

Ritual One

At the end of the guided imagery meditation, play soft, instrumental music. As the group sits in reflective silence, one person quietly brings in dough that is ready for its last kneading. (Fresh dough made by a member of the group has its own symbolic and community value; however, you can use one of a set of small frozen loaves, found in a grocery, which you have defrosted and left to rise. Although kneading commercial dough is not part of the instructions, kneading will not harm it.) The dough should be placed on a breadboard dusted with flour.

After a few minutes of silent reflection, one member of the group goes to the dough and begins to knead it. The person then leaves the room. One by one, each of the others comes forward, kneads the dough, and then leaves the room to continue further reflection.

If Ritual One is to be followed by Ritual Two, bake the bread. *Option:* If this ritual is not to be followed by the second one, members of the group could remain in the room and share their experiences of kneading this bread—what it feels like, what it reminded them of, what it may have symbolized. Close with a spontaneous prayer or a song.

Ritual Two

Place chairs in a circle around a small round table covered with a cloth. A reader may prepare John 6:5–13, adjusting the text for inclusive language.

One person—or several—prepares John 13:14–17; John 13:34–35, and John 15:4–5,7,11,12.

As soft instrumental music is played, members of the group enter the room silently and seat themselves.

The person who prepared John 6:5–13 reads it slowly to the group.

Someone reverently brings in the baked loaf of bread and places it on the table in the center.

Option: A member of the group could "dance" with the bread, lifting it above his or her head, showing it individually to each member of the group, offering it to the north, south, east, and west, and so on. The dancer then places it on the table.

One person—or several—slowly reads the three verses from John.

When the readings are completed, one member takes the loaf of bread from the table, breaks off a piece and gives it to the person on the right. He or she passes the bread to the person on the left who breaks a piece of bread for the person on his or her right and so on. All hold the bread and consume it together.

After meditative silence, all sing "Companions on the Journey" from the album *Companions on the Journey* by Carey Landry; or "Mother Earth," "Come, Spirit," or "We Are the Church" from *WomanSong* by Miriam Therese Winter; or "Dear Sister God" from *Faith Looking Forward* by Brian Wren (see Appendix B).

Option: Some groups may prefer the even greater simplicity of using only the symbols of music, dance, and sharing of the bread.

Option: Light refreshments might be served afterward; for example, serve wine, fruit, cheese, and crackers to continue the celebration of union in Her who gives us our daily food.

Serving Her Through Love and Justice

Opening Prayer

O God, your Son Jesus calls all of us to share bread and wine in memory of Him. He calls all to the table. He excludes none. Widen my vision and my heart so that I can live in that knowledge.

Give me your Spirit so that I may understand what it means to love you, my Mother, with my whole heart and soul and to love my neighbors—my brothers and sisters—as myself. Teach me how to care for my family around the world, how to share what I have. How can I, limited as I am, serve the hungry, the homeless, the poor, the oppressed? Show me what you want me to do to bring about your reign of justice on earth.

You know no hierarchy of persons, but love all of us in a total embrace. Help me to be aware of the ways in which my own racism, sexism, or nationalism keep me separated from those you call me to love. You are, indeed, Mother of us all.

GUIDED IMAGERY MEDITATION

For this prayer, come in fantasy and in spirit to share a meal. You and a group of friends, people who share your journey of faith and service, are planning a celebration of your love and care for one another, of your commitment to each other's good. Each of you will bring gifts of food for a simple meal, gifts that symbolize your willingness to feed one another's spirits, one another's hope and faith and love.

Your group has chosen a place that holds a circular table. Rectangular tables in so many secular and religious celebrations have a head and a foot, an indication in the seating of the superiority of some over others. Your group wants to celebrate the equality of its members and the way God embraces all of Her children with the same unconditional love.

All of your group—women and men—are welcome at this table. What all will celebrate is the relational, nurturing, serving aspects of themselves. So be aware now of your own femininity or feminine side, your willingness to receive another with gentle openness of mind and heart, your desire to leave status and power behind to serve in reverential love. Bring your love for the beautiful details of every day that give simple joy in living.

Find a comfortable yet alert position for this prayer and envision the group with which you will share faith and service at this meal.

Picture the circular table—with chairs around it. What kind of table is it? Wood? Marble? Glass-topped? Elaborate or simple? Walk to it and put your hands on its surface. Run your hands around the edge. Look at the shape of the chairs and feel the material out of which they are made.

What lighting source is in the room? Lamps? Candles? A chandelier? You may look around the room and note a lovely cabinet where the dishes are kept. What else is here? A serving table? Shelves? Do you see any decorations on the walls?

Your gift of service for this meal is to set the table. Remember, this is to be a simple meal, a light meal. Go to the cabinet and take out some plates. Look at one and notice its detail. Place the plates one by one around the table with care and love. Think of your friends who will be using them soon. Feel the shape of the wine glasses as you set one at each place.

Find the cups and saucers and put them to the right of the plates. Now take out the flatware. Notice its pattern. Place each piece carefully and put some serving forks and spoons toward the center of the table. Fold a napkin at each person's place.

Someone else from your group is coming in now, bringing a bottle of sparkling water. The person asks how you are—and means it. So, take a minute to answer that question. How *are* you, right now?

Others are coming in and bringing their gifts of food and drink. They greet each other and show care in some way—by a receptive smile, a caring touch, an affirmation. Watch this happen. Let others greet you and return their greetings in your own loving way.

Everyone is sitting down now. You take a place and sit, too. Someone has set a bowl of fresh flowers in the center of the table. What kind are they? Examine one closely. Reach out and touch it. Look at the whole centerpiece with reverence. Look around the table at the face of each person. Can you meet each one's eyes?

Everyone is about to begin eating. Bow your head in silent prayer. Now one person is getting up and circling the table, offering wine. Watch the flow of the wine as it fills each glass. Everyone is talking quietly, congenially. Another person takes a block of cheese and cuts it into chunks, offering pieces to all

those in reach. You are offered a piece. If you like
cheese, take it and taste it. The plate passes on to
the others. The person who brought the loaf of bread
is tearing off a piece and offering the loaf to you.
Break off a piece for yourself and pass the loaf on to
the person on your right. Watch as he or she accepts
it and tears off another chunk and passes it on to
the next and so on. Watch as it is being offered and
shared around the table. With the others, eat your
part of the bread.

Watch a relish platter being started around
the table by the one who prepared it. Some are
nodding in thanks and in appreciation of its colorful
arrangement. The salad is made of a variety of greens.
The person who brought it inserts a large spoon and
fork and offers the bowl to the others.

Another member of your group comes from the
kitchen with a baked fish on a platter. Watch as this
is passed around the table.

Listen and watch while you and the others
enjoy the food and one another's company. Now,
one of your group is cutting apples and sharing them
around the table. Someone else picks up a bowl of
grapes and offers them to everyone. Smell the coffee
as it finishes brewing. The one who brought it is
beginning to pour some for each person. Another
person is offering baked tarts and another is passing
a dish of homemade candy.

The conversation grows quieter. Everyone at the
table now joins hands and begins to pray to God, to
Her in whom all that is feminine resides and flows.

We thank you for gathering us all together
in your name. We are grateful for Your presence
which we feel as we unite all of our feminine energies in your name. Thank you for your gentle,
and yet electrifying presence, connecting us and
rising from us as we together praise your name.

Thank you for the food you give to us at this table and the food of your word. It is through you that we can share with one another, can nourish each other with both food and your word.

Thank you for your feminine creative love within each of us here, for these reflections of yourself that we see in each other. How wonderful are all the accepting, nurturing, supportive relationships in our lives.

We thank you for our desire to share with others what we ourselves have so that no one and no one's child may be hungry for food or for love.

Gather our energies into yours. Fill us with your Spirit that we may daily nurture your life and your love in all whom we meet.

And now, everyone remains silent and adds prayers of the heart. Add your own personal prayers remaining in gentle communion with Her and with all who share your table.

Suggestions for group leader: Following this meditation, enjoy a simple sharing of food brought by members of the group.

Conclude this meditation with the song "There Is a Feast" from *Cry of Ramah* by Colleen Fulmer (see Appendix B).

Reflection/Discussion Starters

With whom did you share this meal?

What kind of room, furnishings, dishes, flowers did you imagine?

What did you experience as you set the table for your group?

What answer did you give to the question, "How are you?" Did you feel free to answer it honestly?

What form of greeting did you give to your companions?

How did you feel as you met the eyes of each of your companions?

What part of the meal was most significant for you?

How did you feel about holding hands for prayer?

With what parts of the prayer did you most identify?

Were you able to sense God as feminine in this meditation? If so, what helped you to do this?

FOR PERSONAL PRAYER

"Do Not Neglect Hospitality" (Heb 13:2)

These five suggestions for meditation offer you a variety of ways to pray as a welcoming person, to warmly offer both love and justice to the world.

In your imagination, invite a few friends to dinner. Picture them around your table. You still have two empty places.

Option 1:   To fill them, invite two people from a shelter for the homeless. See them with you at the table. Imagine the conversation. How would you treat them, and how might they treat you? How do you feel about having them as guests among your other guests?

Option 2:   Invite two people of a race other than your own and picture them with you around the table. What might you talk about? How do you feel having them as guests?

Option 3:   Invite two people of a different socioeconomic class than yours, either higher or lower. What might lead you to feel comfortable? Or awkward? How do you feel about having them as guests?

Option 4:   Invite two people with disabilities; for example, a person who is blind, hearing-impaired, disabled from polio or some other disease or condition. What special considerations would be needed to make them feel comfortable with you? How do you feel about having them as your guests?

Option 5: Invite two mentally handicapped persons. How might this dinner be different from those above? Might it be easier or more difficult to be a good host or hostess? How do you feel about having the people as your guests?

"Who Is My Neighbor?" (Lk 10:29)

After spending a few minutes relaxing and asking for Her Spirit to open the meaning of the scriptures in your life, read Luke 10:25–37, the Parable of the Good Samaritan.

Consider the people in our country who are born into poverty, then held down by a society that refuses to give them jobs, just wages, or sufficient welfare, that leaves them alone in prisons and shelters through indifference. Consider the people in other countries victimized by Marxist oppression, by totalitarian and military governments, by unethical capitalism, by discrimination and prejudice.

Imagine God in front of you. Be aware of Her love and compassion for all persons. Bring before Her the following people. Picture and give a name to a man or woman or child who represents an oppressed group. For example, Ja and his family who are hunted and driven from the rain forests of Brazil so that industrial countries can turn the forests into grazing ground for cattle that supply meat for fast-food markets; Se, a woman from Nicaragua whose husband has been shot by the Contras because he organized villagers to build a well; Li, a grandmother in Chile who marches around the city square to protest the disappearance years ago of her two sons and a daughter; Chu, 17, who is dying of cancer from pesticides after picking grapes in the migrant worker fields for eleven years; Dick and Tesa, a black couple denied an apartment because of their race; Mark, who is refused work since others discovered he has AIDS; Juan, an 8-year-old Mexican who helps his family survive by salvaging from the garbage dump; Ellen, a divorced mother of three who cannot find a job above minimum wage or one that carries health benefits for herself or her children.

What can you do? Who can you help? Who is your neighbor?

Perhaps you are already donating money or time for the relief of some of your brothers and sisters; perhaps you are working through letters or phone calls to change some unjust system.

Speak with Her who calls you to stop and to help your neighbor.

Psalm Parallel (Psalm 10)

Why, O God, do you not stop
    the deeds that cause destruction?
Arrogantly, the greedy harass the downtrodden,
Who are caught in the systems the rich have contrived.
For greed is turned into virtue
    and the reward of wrongdoing is profits.
Those who win dump contempt on the losers.
"They want to lose. They do not care," they say.
One family becomes homeless, while another buys a yacht.
"They must have deserved it," society says.
"Give us the right to elect our leaders," the peasants cry.
"We must protect our interests," the government says.
"I won't work beside her; she's not of my color."
"Sorry, no work, no help needed here."
"Hire her. Pay less than the minimum wage,
She needs the money and she won't tell."
"We can't afford to filter our waste,
Our product will cost too much."
Rise up, O God, and lift your hand,
Forget not the oppressed.
Why should the indifferent get by with it all
And say, "Why should I worry?"
You do see, you see misery and sorrow
And take them into your hands.
On you the unfortunate depend,
To those without homes, you are a shelter.
Break the strength of the greedy and oppressive,
Give to the hungry their bread.

PERSONAL RITUAL

Choose one action to expand your awareness of those in need. For example:

◆ Visit a shelter for the homeless or a soup kitchen.

◆ Go to a lecture or program on a social justice issue.

◆ Explore a copy of *Sojourners* (an ecumenical monthly magazine exploring faith, politics and culture, published in Washington, D.C.) or *Salt* (a Catholic monthly magazine "for justice-hungry Christians" from Claretian Publications, Chicago) and read at least one article.

◆ If you are ready to do so, copy the Prayer Formula on page 120 and fill it in. Post it where you will see it often or place it inside your bible or another book which you use frequently.

COMMON RITUAL

This ritual is designed for people who have spent a retreat or a day of prayer considering the social justice dimensions of the gospel. Or it can be used by those who have come together to renew their commitments to work for liberation.

Preparation

Four people prepare Matthew 25:31–46 in parts: narrator, king, and two or more of those "sentenced."

Prepare copies of the Reflection Sheet and the Prayer Formula, which appear below. They may be duplicated for one-time use for each person.

Place a large world map on the wall or a large globe on a table.

Ritual

Sing "Come Spirit" from *WomanSong* by Miriam Therese Winter (see Appendix B).

Allow a few minutes of silence followed by the reading of Matthew 25:31–46 in parts.

Take a few more minutes of silence.

Ask for statements of response to the reading. Accept the statements; do not begin a discussion of any of them.

The leader offers the following thoughts in these or similar words:

> All of us here have taken these words of Matthew seriously in our lives. All of us present are offering some response to Jesus' call to feed the hungry, give drink to the thirsty, clothe the naked, and so on. Now is a time to review our responses—to look at the Spirit with which we respond, to ask ourselves honestly if we are doing enough, or to ask ourselves just as honestly if we are doing too much and perhaps not responding to the various hungers and thirsts in our own lives and families. We need to ask ourselves if we are called to continue to respond as we are or to serve in some different way.

> We are going to take some time to consider these questions and I am going to give you a reflection sheet of quotations to use if you wish.

> We will take an extended time to think and pray (thirty to seventy-five minutes). Then we will return and offer the fruits of our reflection by praying together. To help us to do this, I am giving you this prayer formula to consider. It is a prayer through which we can offer our commitments. If you are not ready to offer a commitment or recommitment,

we respect that. Please join the group to add your support for the others.

When you return, bring this formula with you and also some symbol of your commitment to the works of mercy and justice.

Some possible symbols are an orange or any item of food as a sign of sharing food or working for elimination of hunger; a scarf or handkerchief or clothing for providing goods for others; a pencil to symbolize one's voting power; a pen for power to write to the legislature; a newspaper to indicate assuming responsibility to be informed and to vote for those who show concern for justice and for the poor; a watch to signify volunteer time.

When members of the group return, place chairs in a circle around the table holding the globe or in a semi-circle around the map with the table beneath it.

Sing "The Judge's Dilemma" from *The Cry of Ramah* by Colleen Fulmer (see Appendix B). The book accompanying the tape has directions for gestures to accompany words.

A leader says:

> Let's take a few moments of silence.
>
> (Pause one or two minutes.)
>
> We bring our awareness of God's concern for Her poor. We bring our own awareness and concern. We also bring our ability to work toward justice and offer charity. We also bring our limitations.
>
> Let your Spirit move in each of us that we may respond to your promptings within us.

People come forward individually and place a symbol on the table. They use the words of the formula or any spontaneous way of offering themselves. Again, be sensitive to those who are not ready for a commitment or those who prefer to make it in a different way.

Prayer Formula

Each person who chooses to do so says:

I am aware of the sufferings of _____ *(women, men, minorities, abused children, the homeless)* who need _____ *(food, shelter, equal rights, affirmation)* in _____ *(America, South Africa, Ethiopia, Philippines).*

(Point to the place on the map or globe.)

I (re)commit myself to respond to these, my sisters and brothers, by _____. I symbolize my pledge by this _____.

(Place the symbol on the table holding the globe or under the map. *Option:* Pin the Prayer Formula paper on the map at its appropriate place.)

All respond:

We will support your pledge in any way we can.

When the offerings are completed, again ask for brief statements or spontaneous prayer.

Sing "God, Mother of Exiles" from *Cry of Ramah* by Colleen Fulmer; or "One by One" or "Coming Round Again" or "A New Day Dawns" (most suitable for women's groups) from *WomanSong* by Miriam Therese Winter (see Appendix B).

Reflection Sheet

Choose the one or two passages to which you are drawn and hold them in your heart before God. Listen, or bring your request, or ask for enlightenment as you are led to do.

> [God] raises up the lowly from the dust;
> from the dunghill [God] lifts up the
> poor (Ps 113:7).

I have set before you life and death, the blessing and the curse. Choose life, then, that you and your descendants may live" (Deut 30:19).

> The spirit of the Lord GOD is upon me,
> because the LORD has anointed me;
> [God] has sent me to bring glad tidings to
> the lowly,
> to heal the brokenhearted,
> To proclaim liberty to the captives
> and release to the prisoners (Is 61:1).

That I feed the hungry, that I forgive an insult, that I love my enemy in the name of Christ—all these are undoubtedly great virtues. What I do unto the least of my brethren [and sisters], that I do unto Christ. But what if I should discover that the least amongst them all, the poorest of all the beggars, the most impudent of all the offenders, the very enemy himself—that these are within me, and that I myself stand in need of the alms of my own kindness—that I myself am the enemy who must be loved—what then? (C. G. Jung in *Modern Man in Search of a Soul*).

No one can serve two masters. [You] will either hate one and love the other, or be devoted to one and despise the other. You cannot serve God and mammon (Mt 6:24).

[God] has reconciled us to himself [herself] through Christ and given us the ministry of reconciliation (2 Cor 5:18).

Put on the armor of God, that you may be able to resist on the evil day and, having done everything, to hold your ground. So stand fast with your loins girded in truth, clothed with righteousness as a breastplate, and your feet shod in readiness for the gospel of peace (Eph 6:13–15).

You do not need to do extraordinary things. Love those around you (Mother Teresa of Calcutta).

And the fruit of righteousness is sown in peace for those who cultivate peace (Js 3:18).

Above all, let your love for one another be intense, because love covers a multitude of sins. Be hospitable to one another without complaining. As each one has received a gift, use it to serve one another as good stewards of God's varied grace (1 Pt 4:8–10).

Whoever is begotten by God conquers the world. And the victory that conquers the world is our faith. Who [indeed] is the victor over the world but the one who believes that Jesus is the Son of God? (1 Jn 5:4–5).

A young woman was wondering one evening if she was doing enough to care for the poor, to promote their well-being. Pat, one of her children, called to her from the bedroom and asked for a drink of water. The mother took it to her and hugged her another good-night embrace. Pat looked up and said, "Mommy, if you and Daddy didn't feed me, I would die, wouldn't I?"

Note From the Author:

I have written about how our gender images of God affect our society. A similar book could be written on the color of our images of God. What effect does a white God have upon people of color? What effect does such an image have on white people in relationship to people of color? What effect has it had historically?

Or what effect do dominance images of God have upon our society—lord, master, king, judge, almighty ruler? How do more egalitarian images of God affect us—friend, housekeeper, shepherd, forgiving parent, bakerwoman? Does either kind of image "bless" dominance of others in society? If you were using several of these images for God in writing a brief reflection, would you capitalize some and not others? Does that have any implications?

Using feminine images of God in prayer has, I hope, expanded your prayer life and your knowledge of God our Mother, Sister, and Friend. I encourage you to continue praying with feminine as well as masculine images. In addition, I hope you will pursue other images of God, images that reflect God in all our oppressed and dispossessed brothers and sisters.

APPENDIX A

Openers to Connect With One Another

Persons who participate in a day of praying with feminine images of God often come with a friend. Some people are courageous enough to come alone. Rarely does everyone know everyone else. A time for getting acquainted is essential. A good exercise to help people know each other can initiate a climate of openness, humor, and warmth.

Suit one of the following openers to your group.

1) Ask all the members of the group to give their names along with the names of women they admire—one woman per person. The woman may be real or fictional, living or dead, contemporary or historical. Invite them to share reasons for their choices.

2) Ask the members of the group for weather reports along with names; for example, "I am Peggy Carroll and my sky is blue with some wispy clouds on my horizon," or "My name is Jeff Nieman and I am in the middle of a thunderstorm," or "Judy Ipson—some sun is presently breaking through my clouds." Do not ask what the weather represents in their lives. If some begin to explain, accept some brief or light explanations. Do not let anyone get into telling his or her story or unloading problems. (A variation on the weather report is asking the group members what colors [metaphorically] surround them at present.)

3) Ask all participants to introduce themselves by their maternal genealogy—first names only. Thus, "I am Virginia, the daughter of Virginia, and the granddaughter of Anna," or "I am Stephen, the son of Betty, the grandson of Florence." If you wish to add to this, you could ask the members of the group to state a quality they admire in either their mother or grandmother.

4) A leader begins by saying, "My name is *(name)* and there is someone here I would like to get to know (better)." She nods to someone and asks that person to tell her something about his or her life. After doing so, that person says, "My name is . . ."

and chooses someone else. The last person nods to the leader who
began it all.

5) If the group members know each other already, ask them
to tell something about themselves that no one else is likely to
know. For instance, "I read *Gone With the Wind* when I was 13
years old," or "I hate to wash out my stockings at night," or "I've
always wanted to go drag racing," or "I'm always scared when I
begin one of these group things."

6) Ask all the participants to tell about the nicest thing that
happened to them this past week. If you want to add a feminist
touch, you could ask for the best interaction with a woman this
past week. This may have been with a helpful sales clerk, a speaker
who came to a church meeting, one's wife or mother or daughter,
a coworker, a doctor, and so on.

7) Prepare square pieces of cardboard, each with the name of
a well-known woman. The woman may be fictional or real, dead
or alive, contemporary or historical. Fasten a piece of yarn to the
top corners of the cardboard so that it may be hung as a placard
around a participant's neck.

As each participant enters, hang a placard with the cardboard
at her back, name facing out. The participant should not know
the name placed on her. Participants can ask each other questions
about the name on their backs; for instance, "Am I a character in
a novel?" or "Am I a biblical person?" or "Am I alive at present?"
The person asked may answer only "yes," "no," or "I don't know."
A participant can guess the name on her or his back by saying,
"Am I Joan of Arc?" or "Am I Roberta Flack?" If the person ques-
tioned answers "yes," the questioner may turn the placard to the
front.

When all have "discovered themselves" and are seated, ask
the participants to introduce themselves and tell whatever they
may know about their assigned characters.

8) Choose quotations about women—both negative and positive. Type them on strips of paper and cut the strips so that the
first part of the quotation is separate from the second. Put each
half in an envelope. Give all the participants envelopes and in-
struct them to find their other halves. After everyone has done
this and is seated again, the pairs then introduce themselves with

their quotation. Obviously, this activity requires an even number of participants.

Here are some quotations on women to help you begin your own collection:

> I want women to have their rights and while the water is stirring I'll step into the pool.
>> Spoken by Sojourner Truth in 1851 at the Women's Rights Convention

> At present women are taking their places in almost all professions and cultural, social and political institutions as well as in international organizations. Like others, the Catholic woman plays her part in these movements. She cannot and must not evade them.
>> Spoken by Pope Pius XII in 1957 to the World Union of Catholic Women's Organizations

> Man is destined to be a prey to woman.
>> William Makepeace Thackery

> Man and woman are in the image of God, equal in dignity and possessing the same rights.
>> Spoken by Pope Pius XII in 1957 to the World Union of Catholic Women's Organizations

> Blessed art Thou, O Lord . . . for not creating me a woman.
>> Morning prayer of Orthodox Jewish men

> When it is recognized that woman as a person possesses the power to communicate, to integrate, to bring to life, to heal, and to sensitize, a forward step will have been taken toward total humanization of culture.
>> Bishop Carroll T. Dozier, *Intrepid and Loving*, Pastoral letter, Epiphany, 1975

> The whole education of women should be relative to men. To please them, to be useful to them, to win their love and esteem, to bring them up when young, to tend them when grown, to advise and console them; these are the duties of women at all times, and what they ought to learn from infancy.
>> Jean-Jacques Rousseau

If particular care and attention are not paid to the ladies we are determined to foment a rebellion and will not hold ourselves bound to obey laws in which we have no voice or representation.
Abigail Adams

According to the Bible, woman was the last thing God made. It must have been a Saturday night. Clearly, he was tired.
Alexander Dumas

There is no limit to the power of a good woman.
R. H. Benson

Women are the gates of hell.
St. Jerome

No one knows like a woman how to say things which are at once gentle and deep.
Victor Hugo

To be slow in words is a woman's only virtue.
William Shakespeare

Morally, the general superiority of women over men is, I think, unquestionable.
W. E. H. Leckey

I expect that woman will be the last thing civilized by man.
George Meredith

It was to a virgin woman that the birth of the Son of God was announced. It was to a fallen woman that his resurrection was announced.
Fulton Sheen

As regards the individual nature, woman is defective and misbegotten.
St. Thomas Aquinas

Whatever women do, they must do twice as well as men to be thought half as good. Luckily, this is not difficult.
Charlotte Witton

A woman should be covered with shame at the thought that she is a woman.
Clement of Alexandria

The only useless life is woman's.
Benjamin Disraeli

Since women are becoming ever more conscious of their human dignity, they will not tolerate being treated as mere material instruments, but demand rights befitting a human person both in domestic and public life.
> Pope John XXIII in *Pacem in Terris*, no. 41

Women are nothing but machines for producing children.
> Napoleon Bonaparte

Woman is slow in understanding and her unstable and naive mind renders her by way of natural weakness to the necessity of a strong hand in her husband. Her "use" is two-fold: animal sex and motherhood.
> Gregory the Great

Sensible and responsible women do not want to vote.
> Grover Cleveland

Women's sensibility is greater, they are more chaste both in thought and act, more tender to the erring, more compassionate to the suffering, more affectionate to all about them.
> W. E. H. Leckey

It had seemed to me that, considering what St. Paul says about women keeping at home (I have recently been reminded of this and I had already heard of it), this might be God's will. He (the Lord) said to me: "Tell them they are not to be guided by one part of scripture alone, but to look at others; ask them if they suppose they will be able to tie my hands."
> St. Teresa of Avila,
> *Spiritual Revelations: Favors of God*, XIX

In childhood a woman must be subject to her father; in youth, to her husband; when her husband is dead, to her sons. A woman must never be free of subjugation.
> Hindu Code of Manu

Do you not know that you are Eve? . . . You are the devil's gateway. . . . How easily you destroyed man, the image of God. Because of the death which you brought upon us, even the Son of God had to die.
> Tertullian

Where they have not yet won it, women claim for themselves an equality with men before the law and in fact.
> Vatican II, *The Church in the Modern World*, no. 9

It is unchallengeable that woman is destined to live under man's influence and has no authority from her Lord. Woman is something deficient or accidental. For the active power of the male intends to produce a perfect likeness of itself with male sex. If a female is conceived, this is due to lack of strength in the active power, to a defect in the mother, or to some external influence like that of a humid wind from the south.

St. Thomas Aquinas

Among all savage beasts none is found so harmful as woman.

St. John Chrysostom

There is in every true woman's heart, a spark of heavenly fire, which lies dormant in the broad daylight of prosperity, but which kindles up, and beams and blazes in the dark hour of adversity.

Washington Irving

Women are not made to the image of God. I feel that nothing so casts down the manly mind from its heights as the fondling of woman and those bodily contacts that belong to the married state.

St. Augustine of Hippo (354–408)

With respect to the fundamental rights of the person, every type of discrimination, whether social or cultural, whether based on sex, race, color, social condition, language, or religion, is to be overcome and eradicated as contrary to God's intent.

Vatican II, *Gaudium et Spes*, no. 9

Like the universal movements for peace, for amnesty, for justice; the woman's movement is international. Its influence can be a significant factor in the universal proclamation of the Word of God.

Bishop Carroll T. Dozier, *Intrepid and Loving*, Pastoral letter, Epiphany, 1975

For all of you who were baptized into Christ have clothed yourselves with Christ. . . . There is not male and female; for you are all one in Christ Jesus.

Galatians 3:27–28

APPENDIX B

Resource Guide

Resources Recommended Within the Text

Froehle, Virginia Ann, R.S.M. *In Her Presence: Prayer Experiences Exploring Feminine Images of God.* Cincinnati, Ohio: St. Anthony Messenger Press, 1987. A two-tape set of audiocassettes with the guided imagery meditations used in this book.

Fulmer, Colleen. *Cry of Ramah.* An audiocassette and book of songs with dances by Martha Ann Kirk, C.C.V.I. Albany, California: Loretto Spirituality Network, (725 Calhoun Street, 94709), 1990.

Landry, Carey. *Companions on the Journey.* Phoenix, Arizona: North American Liturgy Resources, 1985.

Silvestro, Marsie. *Circling Free.* East Haven, Connecticut: Moonsong Productions, 1983. An audiocassette of women's songs.

Winter, Miriam Therese. *WomanPrayer, WomanSong: Resources for Ritual.* Chicago: Meyer Stone Books, 1987. A book of rituals and songs.

_____. *WomanSong.* Hartford, Connecticut: Medical Mission Sisters, 1987. A set of two audiotapes of the songs from the above book. Tapes, songbook, piano accompaniment, and vocal harmony are available.

Wren, Brian. *Bring Many Names. Faith Looking Forward. Praising a Mystery.* Carol Stream, Illinois: Hope Publishing Company, 1983 to 1989. Three books with hymn texts (with accompaniment) celebrating the biblical calls to justice and equality. Some hymns use feminine images of God.

Other Musical Resources Helpful in Planning Group Prayer or Ritual

Cotter, Jean. *After the Rain.* Chicago, IL: G.I.A. Publications, 1989. An audiocassette of improvised hymns on the piano.

Gardner, Kay. *A Rainbow Path.* Durham, North Carolina: Ladyslipper, Inc., 1984. An audiocassette or recording of instrumental music. Excellent for quiet time during group prayer.

Jones, Michael. Milwaukee, WI: Narada Productions, 1845 N. Farwell Avenue, 53202. Instrumental audiocassettes.

Kobialka, Daniel. Belmont, CA: LiSem Enterprises, Inc., 1775 Old Country Road #10, 94002. Instrumental audiocassettes.

Lanz, David. Narada Productions. See Jones above.

Rowland, Mike. *The Fairy Ring*. Milwaukee, WI: Antiquity Records, 1982. Audiocassette of piano and strings.

Music by George Winston
Check record/tape stores.

Additional artists who have composed and/or performed instrumental music the author has found helpful for quiet time during a group prayer service or ritual are Stephen Halpern, Georgia Kelly, and Zamfir.

Publications Helpful in Planning Group Prayer or Ritual

Amundsen, Sandy, and Irene Moriarty, eds. *Woman-Soul Flowing: Words for Personal and Communal Reflection*. Chicago: The Ecumenical Women's Center, 1978. Words by women for personal and communal reflection.

Gjerding, Iben, and Katherine Kinnamon, eds. *Women's Prayer Services*. Mystic, Connecticut: Twenty-Third Publications, 1983.

Kirk, Martha Ann. *God of Our Mothers*. Cincinnati, Ohio: St. Anthony Messenger Press, 1985. A two-tape set of audiocassettes. Six narrators speak in the persons of eight biblical women.

Kirk, Martha Ann, and Fulmer, Colleen. *Her Wings Unfurled*. Movement and ritual by Kirk, music by Fulmer. Emphasis on justice. Albany, California: The Loretta Spiritual Network, 725 Calhoun Street, 94709, 1990.

Schaffran, Janet, C.D.P., and Pat Kozak, C.S.J. *More Than Words: Prayer and Ritual for Inclusive Communities*. Chicago: Meyer Stone, 1986.

Winter, Miriam Therese. *WomanWord: A Feminist Lectionary and Psalter*. New York: Crossroad Publishing Co., 1990.

Woman's Song. Woman's Song II. Woman's Song III. Chicago: National Sisters Vocation Conference, 1986. A book of prayer services, music, and poetry.

WomanSharing. Cincinnati, Ohio: St. Anthony Messenger Press, 1988. Two-tape set of audiocassettes. Nine women speak of their prayer, their images of God, and their service, which flows from their faith.

General Reference Works on Images
of God and the "Place" of Women

Chicago, Judy. *The Dinner Party*. New York: Anchor Press, 1979.

Luke, Helen. *Woman: Earth and Spirit*. New York: Crossroad Publishing Co., 1985.

Mollenkott, Virginia Ramey. *The Divine Feminine: The Biblical Imagery of God as Female*. New York: Crossroad Publishing Co., 1984. Chapter 15 is particularly useful with regard to scriptural references to eagles.

Schneiders, Sandra. *Women and the Word: The Gender of God in the New Testament and the Spirituality of Women*. New York: Paulist Press, 1986. Considers the way our images of God affect us.

References on the Early History of Worshiping God as Feminine

Hawkes, Jacquetta, and Leonard Wooley. *Prehistory and the Beginnings of Civilization*. New York: Harper & Row, 1963.

James, Edwin O. *The Cult of the Mother-Goddess*. New York: Barnes and Noble, 1959.

———. *The Ancient Gods*. New York: Putnam, 1960.

Jensen, Adolph. *Myth and Cult Among Primitive People*. Chicago: University of Chicago Press, 1963.

Sjoo, Monica, and Barbara Mor. *The Great Cosmic Mother: Rediscovering the Religion of the Earth*. San Francisco: Harper & Row, 1987. On goddess religions of the periods before 2,000 B.C.E.

Stone, Merlin. *The Paradise Papers*. London: Quartel Books, 1976.

———. *When God Was a Woman*. New York: Harcourt, Brace, Jovanovich, 1978. Archeological evidence of the worship of the goddess before (and during) the patriarchal period.

Swanson, Guy E. *The Birth of the Gods*. Ann Arbor, Michigan: University of Michigan Press, 1960.